Discovering
ENGLISH
GARDENS

Kay N. Sanecki

Cover design and line illustrations by Edward Stamp

Shire Publications, Tring, Herts.

© *Kay N. Sanecki 1969*

Bramham Park, Yorkshire

SBN 85263067 0

CONTENTS

Introduction	5
Discovering Gardens	11
Water	16
Garden Buildings	19
The Living Architecture of the Garden	27
Glossary	49
Gardens with Special Features	51
Some Gardens to Visit	58

Stourhead, Wiltshire

Who's Who in stone

Discovering STATUES 4/6
1: Southern England (excluding London)
A pocket guide to the public figures of our town squares, parks and market places
Margaret Baker

Discovering STATUES 4/6
2: Central and Northern England
A pocket guide to the public figures of our town squares, parks and market places
J. D. Bennett

Discovering LONDON 4/6
Statues and Monuments
A guide to over 220 public figures and memorials
Margaret Baker

The hundred years 1830-1930 was a boom time for sculptures of public figures, and in towns all over England statues appeared commemorating the nationally famous or locally worthy. Many of these were by famous sculptors, and some excited considerable comment in their day.

These three books provide a unique guide to the statues of our market squares and public parks.

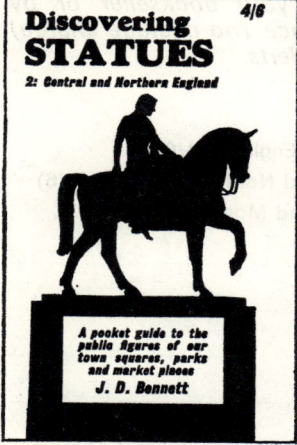

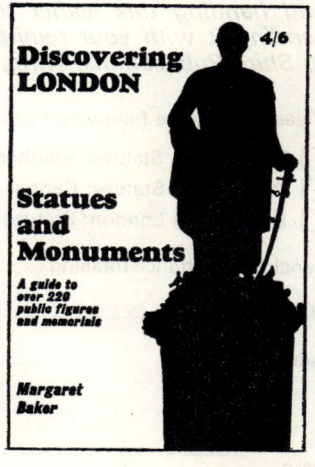

(see over for details)

Discovering Statues: Southern England (4/6)
by Margaret Baker. Arranged geographically by counties and towns, this book concentrates on statues of local worthies, and explains the circumstances leading up to the commissioning of many of them—why Louis XIV lost his head in Yarmouth church, and why Pocahontas is at Gravesend.

Discovering Statues: Central and Northern England (4/6)
by J. D. Bennett. Mr. Bennett covers the counties of Warwicks, Northants, Lincs, northwards, with descriptions of statues from Robin Hood to Titus Salt.

Discovering London: Statues and Monuments (4/6)
by Margaret Baker. Not only the public figures that throng London but many of the commemorative monuments as well are included in this fascinating guide. Little-known statues are included like those of King Alfred [probably the oldest in London] Captain Coram, Dick Whittington and Robert Stephenson, besides all the well-known ones.

You can get your copies of these books by completing and handing this leaflet to your bookseller or by sending it with your remittance (no postage charge) to Shire Publications, Tring, Herts.

Please supply the following books:

☐ Discovering Statues: Southern England (4/6)
☐ Discovering Statues: Central and Northern England (4/6)
☐ Discovering London: Statues and Monuments (4/6)

I enclose remittance totalling ....

Name..

Address ....

....

....

I/3/G

This book does not purport to be a guide book to gardens in England, but is intended to suggest ways in which gardens can be better understood and enjoyed.

INTRODUCTION

Gardens have been made by man for many centuries, sometimes for private enjoyment or as a retreat from the world and at other times as a display of wealth for all the world to admire. We can only read of the gardens of the Chinese empires and of the Ancient World but we can visit and see the gardens men have made in England since medieval times. Botany and gardening came late to these shores, but England quickly became the mecca of botanists and horticulturalists in the seventeenth century and, a hundred years later, many of our finest estates were being laid out on splendidly conceived lines, which were to form part of our landscape. The great eighteenth century gardens have now reached their maturity—and some of them have even passed it or fallen into neglect, and the twentieth century is faced with the necessity of reassessment of these great gardens. Financial resources no longer exist behind many estates to support the necessary staff to maintain the gardens in good condition. Numerous estates have been broken up and redeveloped in the urban planning of the mid-twentieth century; others, like Painshill (Surrey) are in a derelict state and almost beyond rescue. New functions have been found for the houses themselves in numberless instances, such as Stowe (Buckinghamshire) becoming a boys' public school, Shrubland Park (Suffolk) is a health hydro, Lyme Park (Cheshire), Attingham Park (Shropshire) and Ditchley Park (Oxfordshire) are conference centres; Lacock Abbey (Wiltshire) and Wroxton Abbey (Warwickshire) are colleges, both Cliveden (Buckinghamshire) and Dropmore (Buckinghamshire) have been taken recently as American international universities and many mansions have been taken over and are administered by municipal authorities and the gardens turned into public parks.

With the wind of social change has come the acceptance that the public should be given access to many hitherto privately owned gardens. Ownership, be it by a municipal authority, national organisation, private or civic trust, carries some obligation to open the gates to the public, not for inspection, but for enjoyment. As the population explosion continues, open spaces have to be found and preserved for public use and research shows that as gardens are restored, improved or simply saved from the disorder which Nature makes when left to her own devices, more people visit them. Unfortunately, statistics also show that the increase in number of garden visitors is proportionate to the increase in damage done to the gardens, and thus the value of the amenity is not only misunderstood but mis-used. People naturally like to have 'somewhere to go' and set out, not knowing what to expect when they visit these gardens. That there is a need to involve the visitor in an awareness of the meaning of gardens was never more certain than it is today; but it is only by helping him to understand gardens (as opposed to gardening) that there can be a full appreciation of the surroundings. One hopes that with a little more knowledge the visitor will not only derive increased enjoyment but also not mis-use other people's gardens.

A garden open to the public, be it large or small, is really not the place to set up the stumps and arrange a family cricket match—although this activity is becoming quite commonplace on many stately lawns! This little book sets out to explain not only how the various kinds of gardens have come about, how they reflect social history and taste, but what to look for and how to interpret it in order that the fullest benefit may be derived from every hour of garden gazing.

Garden Cities

As a nation we have developed a sensitivity towards gardens and regard our own, be it 'pocket handkerchief' or manorial estate, as something highly personal, but tend to take for granted the provision of gardens for public use. The fashioning of suitable surroundings for contemporary architecture requires consideration and for the older members of the community a reassessment to 'get one's eye in' to the new concepts in design. Public gardens and municipal parks generally, used to be sombre shrubberies, duck ponds and band stands, but now the creation of space—or at least the illusion of space—and scale—are the major considerations and require the specialized attention of the landscape architect. The importance of plants for their suitability to prevailing conditions is a twentieth century manifestation, stemming strongly from the work of Gertrude Jekyll (1843-1935) and William Robinson (1838-1935). The employment of foliage form as well as effectiveness during the flowering season can be enjoyed in most municipal gardens today. The restfulness, the very permanence of a garden, can become part of the daily life of towns and cities, and there is no need to travel miles to some famous garden to start one's discovery of gardens.

A sensitivity to colour and general design, a pause to ask

oneself *how* each public garden has been conceived, is the simple beginning of appreciation and coupled with a flexibility of thought will lead to an inexhaustible source of pleasure and knowledge.

Gardens as landmarks, as waiting areas or a lunch-time rendezvous are common to every city but are dependent upon the wealth and space available and differ widely from one municipality to the next. Excellent public gardens are a feature of such places as Cheltenham, Bath, Torquay, Bournemouth, Brighton, Southport, Stratford-on-Avon, Norwich, Leamington Spa and Harrogate, and the conception of the so-called garden city following the urban development of Bournville and such places as Letchworth has revolutionised what one has come to expect in newly established communities.

City Gardens

A remarkably high proportion of city gardens are of ecclesiastical origin, not only the churchyard gardens and cathedral precincts but such plots as the college gardens of Oxford and Cambridge and the Temple Gardens, Highgate Wood, and Queens Park, Kilburn, in London owe their foundation to monastic settlements. The City of London now administers seventy open spaces within the square mile; some the natural outcome of heavy bombing are now included in the replanning of the city, opening up new vistas of some old city buildings. The burden of something in excess of £30,000 a year required to maintain these plots, is drawn from the Rates Fund. The gardens include St. Paul's Garden, St. Paul's churchyard, Bunhill Fields, Finsbury Circus Garden, and Postmen's Park. By an Act of Parliament in 1878 the Corporation of the City of London was authorised to acquire land within 25 miles of the City, to be preserved and maintained for recreation and such areas as Epping Forest, Burnham Beeches and Highgate Wood are under its administration. The current shift of responsibility for many of London's open spaces under the London Government Act 1963 will not in any way impede the public access and the general amenities afforded.

A number of London Square gardens mainly in Kensington and Chelsea are still privately owned and the general public do not have access to the keys. Although for "residents only" it is interesting to note that in the heart of London, where land is so scarce, a new square, Woodsford Square, has been made on the once estate of Holland House.

Trees are a distinguishing feature of some squares, like

the strangely buttressed London planes in Berkeley Square, and there are other giant planes in Bedford Square.

The London parks in the past were all private estates or Royal Parks. Kensington Park and Chiswick were redesigned by William Kent, some of the avenues of trees still remaining in the former were designed by him and the park has been open to the public since the summer of 1839. It was Queen Victoria who first allowed public access to Kensington Gardens, Hampton Court and Kew and the gardens were declared "open all the year round, to all respectably dressed persons, from sunrise to sunset." Kensington Gardens have remained the playground of children in both fact and fancy and the irresistible attraction of water draws thousands of visitors yearly. These London parks, and all municipal parks, are open all the year round and are faithfully maintained in all seasons. The true garden visitor continues his interest in winter gaining varied enjoyment from 'the park' merely as an open space of immense beauty in frost and snow or as a place of pilgrimage to see the early spring daffodils.

Country Gardens

Similar estates or parks exist all over the country, and even where urban development has clutched at them a nucleus of the former expanse remains used as a public park. Cassiobury Park in Watford prevented development of the town to the west as long as the Capel family held it, but now redeveloped, the 'park' is a fragment of its former size.

Having been persuaded to reconsider public gardens the awareness of gardens becomes more pronounced and considerable aesthetic pleasure is to be gained from the contemplation of planning of any number of such plots. Country railway stations, and fire stations, garages, roundabouts, lock gardens provide a series of oases, some of them unexpectedly delightful—but notably absent altogether at airports. Pub gardens, large or small have developed from the privet and privy plots to areas of charm designed to attract custom, in a motor-car age. Their extent in many instances is dependent only upon the provision of an adequate car park! Many pub gardens change in attraction with the managers or owners of the public house itself, but such places as The Park, Nr. Derby with its sunken rose garden, the terraced rock gardens of The Royal Oak in Brownhills, the Golden Cross at Marlbrook and the Rose Revived at Pishill (Oxfordshire) are worth a visit. At Tonbridge, The Cardinal's Error has a garden reputed to be 400 years old and age is the keynote in many of the city pub gardens, notably in cathedral cities.

Most people have their favourite pub with a garden, tucked away along some country lane. The Bull's Head at Loughborough is remarkable and probably unique for its courtyard and water garden—almost like a winter garden within the hotel—in the heart of the town. Many tiny yards are turned into attractive outdoor 'bars' as at The Bear Hotel at Marlborough. Others, though not open for public use, provide daily enjoyment, perhaps near a bus stop like The Railway Hotel at Boxmoor (Hertfordshire) and The Railway Hotel at Petersfield (Hampshire) both of which display colourful bedding schemes. Hotels and restaurants with gardens are legion but the gardens of Charney Manor (Berkshire) and Gravetye Manor (Sussex) are especially interesting. The former is an old manor house built about 1260 and is the earliest known example of an open-plan manor house still extant. The walled garden boasts many unusual shrubs. The garden at Gravetye Manor, on the other hand, is open only to residents of the hotel but it was the home of William Robinson 'The Father of English Gardening' and many of his favourite plants, particularly wall plants, are to be seen there.

The combination of restaurant with garden is treated in vastly different ways but reaches its most fascinating in the roof gardens of Derry and Toms (Kensington) and Harveys (Guildford). The former is a so-called period garden, formal in conception, enclosed and restful. In Guildford the treatment is totally different, the breeze snaps at the troughs and trees but the small water garden, though busy, is enchanting.

Urban 'ribbon' development tends to provide a track of continuous (but mixed!) garden between carriageway and dwelling, sometimes providing landmarks. But the gardens of the older and humbler homes have often remained untouched by fashion and the English cottage garden may not be just the figment of the calendar. Tiny Cornish cottages bedecked with fuchsias, the cottages of the Isle of Wight, surrounded by fluffy hydrangeas, or Lakeland stone houses supporting roses may each have their vernacular architecture enhanced by widely differing gardens. A true cottage garden is rather hard to find, one perhaps looks for the reproduction of Anne Hathaway's cottage at Stratford-on-Avon but one of the best, full of interesting "cottage garden plants" is at Lye End, Woking (Surrey). A cottage garden richly stocked, on a larger and more sophisticated scale, is East Lambrook Manor (Somerset).

Cemeteries used to represent perpetual bereavement but the crop of Gardens of Remembrance adjoining the crematoria are outstanding examples of a twentieth century approach to garden form, and not just moribund plots.

Thus the everyday observation of gardens and the use to which they are put is the first important stage in discovery.

Beyond this, curiosity leads us on to other peoples' gardens. Many private gardens are open especially during the summer months, usually for charity. They reflect faithfully the interest of their owners, or of previous owners and the visitor, however ignorant of the finer arts of garden design would do well to respect the use to which these gardens are put.

In all parts of the country, plant nurseries are open to the public from time to time and the visitor who has an inquiring mind about plants can often find much to interest him there. Garden centres, a post-war phenomena in Britain, provide interest of a less aesthetic nature but are a fairly accurate reflection of the way in which the horticultural trade is up dating itself to the demands of the mid-twentieth century.

A cardinal rule, and one so often overlooked, is to allow sufficient time to see and—if necessary to return to—whatsoever one may find of special interest in a garden. And, it need hardly be said not to go in August expecting to see the rhododendrons or in April to find the herbaceous borders in full effect. Sometimes a garden acquires a reputation for roses or spring bulbs, or autumn colour and this should never deter the visitor from going at some other time of year as well, should the occasion present itself. A garden is a changing spectacle, not only from season to season but from morning to evening as the shadows play and the reflections change— a point upon which photographers will arrange the time of their visit.

Palladian bridge at Wilton House, Wiltshire.

DISCOVERING GARDENS

The discovery of gardens is the discovery of pleasure, not only in the personal enjoyment afforded by visiting gardens, but in the reflection that since the Renaissance 'pleasure gardens' have been part of the English way of life. The visitor must learn to regard a garden, whatever the size, as an art form—a finished piece of work—rather than a practical exercise in gardening. Naturally one muses upon the sheer mechanics of the building of some of the great landscape gardens of the seventeenth and eighteenth centuries, when devoid of mechanical means, gangs of workers set about making lakes, constructing terraces and courtyards with unimaginably crude and heavy implements. One must enter the scene as a whole, absorb the atmosphere and consider the design and form, background, reflections, textures, all of which play a part in forming the general picture. Gardens are like rooms in that they can be an expression of their owners taste, wealth, interests and even dreams. And often as the impact of a room can be immediately attractive, so one can discover a spontaneous sympathy with a garden—and sometimes return again and again always to rediscover it as a work of art.

What to Expect

A good garden visitor is like a good driver—he expects the unexpected. An imaginary picture is often formed of a garden about which one has read or heard or even seen photographs, but the instant of arrival there banishes all the previous ideas and the garden is 'not at all what I expected'. Period will give a hint of what can be expected as will size and aspect. Generally it can be assumed that the larger garden becomes known as a 'water garden', 'rose garden', 'woodland garden' or 'landscape garden' but this is only a very comprehensive name. Frequently the general guides to gardens open to the public are guilty of labelling a garden in this way and the visitor arrives only to find much more of charm or interest than the lilacs or autumn colour he has been briefed to expect.

It is on the interpretation of the various features that go to make garden design, that most enjoyment is to be derived. No one can hope to understand everything in a season or two of garden visiting, and discovery is never complete but is a continual pleasure. The individual plants and planting schemes are there for the benefit of the connoisseur and to delight the eye; and getting to know plants is another subject in itself. But the colour and texture and type of plant is the very fabric with which the garden picture is painted and atmosphere created. Naturally, shade loving woodland plants like primulas, lilies and hostas must not be expected in a garden on a baked chalk hillside, and sub-tropical bedding is not likely ever to be found on the exposed Pennines. The greatest distinction in type to be found between one garden and another is the formal and informal design. It is possible to find both styles in the same garden.

Formal Gardens

The earliest gardens in England were always constructed on formal lines, with regular geometric patterns. Rectangular plots enclosed by yew, box, hornbeam or holly hedges—some low and some mighty—formed the basic pattern of many gardens. In Elizabethan times terraces, clipped hedges and topiary were the fashion and the whole atmosphere was one of organisation and regularity. The most charming remaining example is at Montacute (Somerset) where a sunken lawn is bordered by formally clipped evergreens and has at the centre a geometrically designed lily pool surrounded by a balustrade, added in 1894. The long terrace under the north walk of the house commands views over the surrounding countryside. The 'courtyard' garden, now grassed over but for a gravel path round the perimeter, was the original courtyard entrance to the house at the east. At each corner is a pavilion and the surrounding walls are ornamented in a manner typical of the period and include two gazebos.

Other houses built at the same time, such as Hatfield House (Hertfordshire), Burghley (Northamptonshire), Knole (Kent), Burton Agnes (Yorkshire) and Astley Hall (Lancashire) have no remains of the gardens that must have surrounded them then. Formality of the period is to be found, however, at Hampton Court (Middlesex) where Cardinal Wolsey made the first great garden of the period complete with terraces, topiary and a maze, and was to be emulated to a greater or lesser degree by numerous Tudor landowners.

Formal treatment, in which man directed how Nature survived, remained the favourite style of gardening, varying with French, Italian and Dutch influence according to the taste of the day. When for instance the exiled court of Charles II returned from France on the Restoration in 1660 the French style of gardening became the vogue here among the aristocrats and examples of the style can be seen at Blickling (Norfolk), Melbourne (Derbyshire), and Chatsworth (Derbyshire) though these gardens are not as they were laid out and have been 'improved' by subsequent generations.

The seventeenth century brought a spate of smaller manor house gardens, all planned on formal lines, some of them intricate and overpowering by present day standards. Topiary reached its apogee, high hedges, avenues, statuary, knot gardens and parterres abounded with all that is associated with Jacobean gardens. The new seventeenth century garden at the Royal Botanic Gardens, Kew is a good present day reconstruction of what gardens of the period were like. With the arrival of William and Mary to the throne in 1689 the Dutch influence of the Court was reflected on our gardens for people naturally decorated their houses and gardens with reminders of their native customs. Probably the best example of a Dutch garden of the period is to be seen at Westbury Court (Gloucestershire). Here is a remarkable water garden in the Dutch style. Construction began in 1698 by Col. Maynard and was finished by his widow after his death. The house no longer remains, but at present the garden is being renovated and reconstructed by the National Trust. The Garden History Society has advised on the replanting and it is hoped that a replica can be achieved bearing close similarity to the original. The water works have been found to be in working order, so the task of dredging and renovating the canal walks has been justified. The calm water will again reflect the holly and yew hedges as it was planned to do in Maynard's time. The pavilion at the head of the canal is being rebuilt, as an almost exact replica of the original. The works can be seen in progress from a lay-by at Westbury-on-Severn on the Chepstow road out of Gloucester, the A.48, and the National Trust plans to open the gardens to the public on completion of the work.

From the sixteenth century onwards, as the great trade routes of the world were opened, many new plants and horticultural techniques reached England and she quickly became the great centre of botany and gardening for Europe—and indeed through the centuries whenever the English speaking peoples have colonised they have made gardens. Formality was the only known form of garden until such men as William Kent and the notorious 'Capability' Brown swept it aside in the eighteenth century. It returned in an elaborate vogue during Victorian days in villa gardens and is now used only to set off plants themselves as in many modern rose-gardens and in the colourful seasonal bedding schemes of public parks to-day,

Examples of formal gardens: Buscot (Berkshire), Wrest Park (Bedfordshire), Lanhydrock House (Cornwall), Montacute

(Somerset), Hutton-in-the-Forest (Cumberland), Chatsworth (Derbyshire), Haddon Hall (Derbyshire), Hardwick Hall (Derbyshire) and Hatfield House (Hertfordshire).

Informal Gardens

Until the mid-eighteenth century there had been no such description as 'formal' for gardens because every design had been regularly laid out in some geometric way, but taste was to change. The architect William Kent turned his creative flair to gardens and broke away from the tortured formality of previous years. Inspired by the Italian landscape and landscape painters Kent laid out several new landscape gardens. The one that remains virtually unchanged is Rousham (Oxfordshire). Here the winding river Cherwell is used as a setting for the green landscape garden with its wooded walks, groups of trees and temples. Rousham is interesting in that the estate still belongs to the same family that commissioned Kent's work and the pre-Kent part of the garden contains one of the loveliest dovecotes in England. (It has been renovated recently).

At the time Kent was working there began a great swing towards the natural or informal garden and three of the greatest ever to mantle the English hills came into being during the eighteenth century. Painshill (Surrey), Stourhead (Wiltshire) and Stowe (Buckinghamshire). The first alas has fallen into utter decay. Stourhead, "the greatest park in England" is administered by the National Trust and Stowe is a boys' public school. It was at Stowe while working for Lord Cobham that Lancelot ('Capability') Brown learned his trade which not only brought him immortality but was to change the face of the English landscape.

Brown swept aside the ordered regimented plants and masonry. He dammed rivers to make lakes, moved earth to form hills, planted trees in groups, took paths winding over the lawns and literally brought the countryside up to the windows of the house.

As the nineteenth century advanced there was a considerable swing to smaller gardens, Humphrey Repton who followed Brown as a landscape gardener introduced small intimate gardens to afford some privacy, some variety, and to make the garden around the house a more personal possession. Examples can be seen at Ashridge (Hertfordshire) where the rose garden, the monks' garden and the Italian garden are all attributed to Repton ; and at Sheringham Park (Norfolk) and Tatton Park (Cheshire).

During Victorian times much intricate bedding out of plants was practised, echoing the formality of the sixteenth and seventeenth centuries, but the grottos, ferneries, rustic work provided the period's own type of informality. When at the turn of the present century William Robinson campaigned for the abolition of the last vestige of Victoriana, informal gardens as we know them today came into being with the herbaceous border, the woodland garden, the water and rock garden.

Examples of nineteenth century informal gardens can be seen at Killerton (Devon), Wisley (Surrey), Biddulph Grange (Staffordshire), Muncaster Castle (Cumberland), Hughenden Manor (Buckinghamshire), Ascott (Buckinghamshire), Ketteringham Hall (Norfolk), Sandringham House (Norfolk), Bristol Zoological Gardens, Alton Towers (Staffordshire) and Birmingham Botanic Gardens (Warwickshire).

Duncombe Park, Yorkshire.

WATER

Probably the most universal feature found in gardens of all periods, whatever the scale and design, is water. It can be used in one of two ways, still and calm when it "reflects the sky" and colour and adds to the expanse of the garden, or splashing and wandering along to provide movement and gaiety. Smooth areas of water be they formal or informal in concept will always emphasise the quietness of a garden. Informal lakes are to be seen at such places as Stourhead (Wiltshire) and Sheffield Park (Sussex)—where the main feature is five large lakes which come to life among the autumn colour for which the park is famous; Hodnet Hall (Shropshire) has delightfully picturesque lakes; at Blenheim Palace (Oxfordshire) the river was dammed by 'Capability' Brown to make the most natural of lakes; Blickling Hall (Norfolk) has perhaps the most perfectly landscaped lake in England; Clumber Park (Nottinghamshire), Chartwell (Kent), and Nostell Priory (Yorkshire) where one can try one's hand at the oar or tiller. Formal water can be used to emphasise a design as at Buscot Park (Berkshire), Wrest Park (Bedfordshire), Westbury Court (Gloucestershire), Bramham Park (Yorkshire) or Chatsworth (Derbyshire) and are known as **canals** when used in this way. Burnby Hall (Yorkshire) has one of the most remarkable artificial pools for sheer size. Two pools cover a combined area of more than 2 acres, an upper water and, 10ft. below, a lower water built in 1903-1910 at a cost then of £8,000. Many kinds of water lilies flourish there and there is interesting marginal planting as well. The time to visit Burnby Hall is in high summer not only for the water lilies but for the cricket which is played on the green bordering the pools. The nearby church tower completes the village green atmosphere.

Moats, usually relics of medieval times, are used as garden features at Ludstone Hall (Shropshire), Blickling (Norfolk), New Hall ((Warwickshire) and Hever Castle (Kent). At Hever the walls of the castle are tastefully clothed with climbing plants which reflect in the moat making a remarkable garden feature.

An artificial lake in the form of a swan is to be found at West Wycombe Park (Buckinghamshire) but a **swan pool** can be seen at Emmanuel College Garden (Cambridgeshire) and Trebatha (Cornwall)—a garden in which water plays a great part in the design, as waterfalls and cascades are set in a naturally wooded site. Black swans are a feature at Chartwell (Kent) and Wakehurst Place (Sussex).

Waterfalls are generally associated with rock work, as at the Royal Horticultural Society's Garden at Wisley (Surrey), a rock garden recently reconstructed on the site of the old one; at Sezincote (Gloucestershire), where Humphrey Repton designed the 'first rock garden', the present-day planting scheme is the work of Graham Thomas. At Buckhurst Mill (Berkshire) there are again waterfalls in the woods and a series of cascades terraced down to a lake. The most magnificent cascades and waterfalls are at Chatsworth (Derbyshire) where the Great Cascade emanates from the Cascade House through several sources and tumbles down a series of steps on the Derbyshire hillside. Elsewhere, the Emperor Fountain throws a jet of water into the air which reaches 276 ft on a calm day. It was designed by Joseph Paxton when he was almost unknown, and he was later to design the Crystal Palace based on the lines of the great Conservatory he built at Chatsworth. Similar single-jet **fountains** are a feature of modern gardens. There is one at Welwyn Garden City, installed to commemorate the Coronation of Queen Elizabeth II in 1953 and an attractive one in the Water Garden at Hemel Hempstead, designed by Geoffrey Jellicoe. Examples of more elaborate fountains, combined with some statuary (sometimes to house the waterworks!) are at Ascott (Buckinghamshire), Waddesdon Manor (Buckinghamshire), the Perseus Fountain at Witley Court (Worcestershire), Ammerdown Park (Somerset), the Pagan Fountain at Holkham Hall (Norfolk) and the Sea Lion Fountain at Julians (Hertfordshire). The association of goldfish with fountain basins in garden design started about 200 years ago, purely for ornamental purposes. Prior to that fish ponds had housed carp for consumption and 'tanks' were invariably associated with the gardens on monastic sites. A modern version can be seen at St. Paul's Waldenbury (Hertfordshire) and much older ones at Castle Ashby ((Northamptonshire) and at Arlington Mill (Gloucestershire). Monastic sites were inevitably associated with a river; many remain as gardens bordering the **river** as at Bisham Abbey (Berkshire) one time home of Anne of Cleves; the Temple Gardens, London where the Knights Templars built a huge monastery by the river; the Forbury Gardens, where fragments remain of Reading Abbey, once the largest in England. Also at Fountains Abbey (Yorkshire)—now part of Studley Royal and at Forde Abbey (Dorset). But the incorporation of a river into a garden scheme gives a great sense of permanence to a garden, whether it be as a distant view or borrowed landscape as at

Cliveden (Buckinghamshire) and Nuneham Court (Oxfordshire) —at present undergoing restoration and to be opened to the public in two or three years time—and Charlecote Park (Warwickshire); or as part of the garden itself as one finds at Chiswick Park (London), Rousham (Oxfordshire), Clare College (Cambridge), Wilton House (Wiltshire) or the Oxford Botanic Garden.

The remains of **bath houses** are to be seen occasionally and always arouse much curiosity in the visitor and not a little astonishment that earlier generations should have bathed out of doors. Forerunners of the present-day vogue for swimming pools in the garden, bath houses provided for splashing about (but not swimming) in cold water. At Packwood House (Warwickshire) the remains of such a pool are to be seen, but the most elaborate example is at Wrest Park (Bedfordshire). This 'building' has been recently renovated and is in a secluded part of the garden providing privacy for the bathers. The house is roofed in, has an antechamber and steps and 'seats' around the pool itself.

A variety of design is to be found in **bridges** of stone or wood but the three most noteworthy are the Palladian bridges at Wilton House (Wiltshire), Stowe (Buckinghamshire) and The Priory Garden (Bath). Palladianism is an architectural style which crept into landscape adornment at the time of William Kent and apart from the house itself at Holkham Hall (Norfolk) it is evident at Rousham (Oxfordshire) where Kent added the Praeneste arcade in Palladian style.

Rousham, Oxfordshire

GARDEN BUILDINGS

The provision of pleasure is the only function of the various garden buildings; pleasure either as leisure and somewhere to go to sit or as visual delight. A temple, pavilion or garden house glimpsed among trees is merely an aesthetic enjoyment of the picture created within the garden.

As **temples** they were built to adorn the eighteenth century landscapes and are usually round, rectangular or octagonal with elaborate porticos, Corinthian pillars and domes. They serve no purpose other than to carry the eye along a vista, to enhance the pastoral scene and to add a point of interest to the landscape. Such buildings can be seen at their best at Stourhead (Wiltshire), Stowe (Buckinghamshire), Castle Howard (Yorkshire), Studley Royal (Yorkshire) and also at Alton Towers (Staffordshire), St. Paul's Waldenbury (Hertfordshire), Duncombe Park (Yorkshire), West Wycombe Park (Buckinghamshire), Lee Ford (Devon) by Adam, Stancombe Park (Gloucestershire), Hidcote Manor (Gloucestershire), and down the architectural scale to garden houses of various forms. Perhaps the most noteworthy are at Killerton (Devon) where the floor is of tree trunks, at Bicton Gardens (Devon) where deer bones are incorporated in the decoration, at Abbotswood (Gloucestershire), at Ascott (Buckinghamshire) with memorial plaques to two sons, Antony and Evelyn, at Tintinhull (Somerset) as part of the formal water garden, and at Wrest Park (Bedfordshire) as the Bowling Green House, recently restored. At Bressingham Hall (Norfolk) there is a charming circular garden house of flint and thatch. Sometimes one finds these garden houses incorporated in the wall surrounding the enclosed garden, the best examples are at Montacute (Somerset). At Packwood House (Warwickshire) there is what might be supposed to be such a garden house of eighteenth century design but upon examination it is found to house the furnaces that provided heat for the cavity walls surrounding the garden so that not only could fruit be protected from frost but vines and peaches could be grown without difficulty, out of doors.

Orangeries

One of the first exotic plants to be cultivated here was the orange, during the late sixteenth and seventeenth centuries, and the necessity to provide protection from our climate, particularly in winter, resulted in the construction of some lavish and functional buildings. Many nowadays are in ruins, or at best in a state of neglect, but nevertheless some fine examples are still to be found, in some instances, as at Sezincote (Gloucestershire) and Ashridge (Hertfordshire), an integral part of the house. Their former magnificence and adornment was undoubtedly a display of wealth and the facilities afforded for growing additional tender exotic plants were soon apparent and as fashion and necessity dictated the furnishing of conservatories came about—their apogee probably amid Edwardian festoonery. Some of the gardens in which orangeries can be seen are Wrest Park (Bedfordshire), now a restaurant, Ammerdown Park (Somerset), Saltram House (Devon), Rudding Park (Yorkshire), Heveningham Hall (Suffolk), Hampton Court (London) and at the Royal Botanic Gardens, Kew (Surrey). **Greenhouses** set apart for the cultivation of fruit are now few and far between, the high cost of maintaining them is more uneconomical in an age when fresh fruit is readily available on the market. But orchard houses, as they were called, specially constructed for the cultivation of vines, or peaches and nectarines or even apples and pears can be seen at Luton Hoo (Bedfordshire), Waterperry Horticultural School (Oxfordshire), Dunsborough Park (Surrey) and Petworth House (Sussex) among other places.

Walls

The use of **walls** to provide protection for tender plants is a common horticultural practice and the selection of the aspect, say a south or south-west facing wall, is often the criterion of success with tender shrubs. Numberless examples are to be seen when visiting other people's gardens and it always adds to the interest to note the age of the plant and the aspect of the wall. But **walled gardens** proper are a source of endless information to the visitor with the enquiring mind and a little imagination! Materials vary from district to district and designs of the coping are sometimes picturesque, as in Dorset and Somerset where tiles and thatch are set like little eaves along the wall. Walled gardens have existed ever since the cultivated land was outside the 'keep' of the medieval homestead, in the first place walled for possession and latterly walled for protection from the elements, vandals and animals. At Croft Castle (Herefordshire) the walled kitchen garden is run on the old economic lines and provides a good example for the visitor to study the planting schemes and methods. Many examples are to be found of walled kitchen and flower gardens set apart from the main 'pleasure' grounds, obviously maintained in days gone by (if not today) to provide food for the estate. At Tew Park (Oxfordshire) there is a series of walled gardens, and good stone walled gardens are to be seen at Athelhampton (Dorset) and Lacock Abbey (Wiltshire). Others are to be seen at Fawnlees Hall (Co. Durham), Theydon Priory (Essex), Houghton Lodge (Hampshire), Belmont Park (Kent), Stanhope Hall (Norfolk), Easton Neston (Northamptonshire), Foston Old Rectory (Yorkshire), Julians (Hertfordshire), Broadlands (Hampshire), Glenham Hall (Suffolk) and at Wrest Park (Bedfordshire)—the latter now used to house much experimental work but open to the public when the National Institute of Agricultural Engineering has its open days.

Serpentine or 'crinkle crankle' walls which are walls built along a wavy line are sometimes to be found, notably in Sussex, Oxfordshire and the west country.

The so-called walled-garden is not always used for cultivating fruit and vegetables but can enclose a rose garden as at Kelvedon Hall (Essex) or a large formal garden like the one at Raby Castle (Co. Durham). At Nymans (Sussex) the walled garden is formal in design, a stone urn and miniature pool at the centre, flanked by four clipped yews with topiary finials. Again at Polesden Lacey (Surrey), the old-world rose garden within brick and flint walls has rustic pergolas, informally paved paths bordered by lavender hedges. Occasionally it may simply be a garden enclosed by walls of ancient buildings as some of the college gardens of Oxford and gardens in cathedral precincts. The old walled garden at the Deanery, Sonning (Berkshire) is all that remains of the Bishop's Palace of the See of Wessex, while at the other end of the scale a modern wall, built entirely by the present owners, is to be found at Alderley Grange (Gloucestershire). Wall building, and bricklaying was a relaxation and pastime for the late Sir Winston Churchill who built his kitchen garden wall at Chartwell (Kent). At Alton Towers (Staffordshire) the scallop-top wall is of particular interest.

In some instances the enclosed garden is a **courtyard garden**. Relic of a domestic requirement of former centuries the courtyard has either been made into a garden or is decorated with plants in a simple way—say in tubs and other containers as at Tintinhull (Somerset) or with clipped shrubs as at Wayford Manor nearby. At Barrington Court (Somerset) a fountain plays in the centre of the court and at Hardwick Hall (Derbyshire), while at Haseley Court (Oxfordshire) the courtyard is turved, with an astrolobe in the centre. Nymans (Sussex), where the walls of the old world house are clothed with plants that survived the fire, has perhaps the most enchanting courtyard garden of all, bordering the house on one side and grassed over in sections intersected by stone paved paths.

At Cottesbrook Hall (Northamptonshire) in 1930 the old courtyard (or forecourt) at the back of the house was 'improved' by two curving walls connecting the main block to two small partitions, and the entrance of the house moved round to this new turved courtyard.

Boundary walls of enormous proportion built at considerable cost enclose many estates, some of them with the date of construction worked into the wall itself, as at Hartwell House (Buckinghamshire). The varying design of gates provides much of interest, though it is sad to see so many in a state of disrepair. Lodges, quite often in pairs and of remarkably different design, were the homes of the gatekeepers whose duty it was to open and close the gates twenty four hours a day, as required. The older gatehouses, partially fortified in some cases, usually spanned the entrance and the best example is at Lanhydrock (Cornwall). The existing examples of gate houses of many designs provide another interest for the garden visitor, and can be seen at many places—often at the roadside —when driving. Note those at Blenheim Palace (Oxfordshire), the Botanic Garden (Oxford), Charlecote (Warwickshire), Cranborne Manor (Dorset), Castle Howard (Yorkshire), Mentmore (Buckinghamshire), Cerne Abbas (Dorset), and Groombridge Place (Kent). Elsewhere they are all that remains of a former garden as at Hampstead Marshall (Berkshire) and Holdenbury (Northamptonshire).

Lower walls are frequent features of many gardens, either as retaining walls for banks or for completion of a **terrace.** Balustrades usually of stone but sometimes of lead or ironwork decorate these terrace walls and bear a vast assortment of finials and other ornament along their length. Urns, lions, statuary, plant containers of varying kinds, lamps, foliage, serpents, little lead gods, horses—the collection is extensive or selective and can all be found perching on walls. Modern terracing does not seem to require this type of adornment but many of the grander gardens of the eighteenth century and nineteenth century built on sloping sites are terraced elaborately. Ornate balustrades and flights of steps of Hollywood-like proportions can be seen at such locations as Harewood House (Yorkshire), Shrubland Park (Suffolk), Trentham Park (Staffordshire), Chatsworth (Derbyshire), Haddon Hall (Derbyshire), Castle Howard (Yorkshire), Rous Lench Court (Worcestershire), Cliveden (Buckinghamshire) and Hatfield House (Hertfordshire).

Dovecotes

Dovecotes were built to house pigeons and were introduced into Britain by the Normans. In the seventeenth century it was estimated that there were some 26,000 dovecotes in this country and at that time the pigeon was an important item in the winter diet. Fresh meat was not obtainable especially towards the end of the winter because cattle could not be kept, other than for breeding purposes. About the 1730's a man who earned himself the name of 'Turnip' Townsend, improved the production of mangolds and turnips thus providing winter fodder for the animals, and from the mid-eighteenth century pigeon husbandry declined. Unfortunately the comparatively few remaining dovecotes are in a state of disrepair though restoration is taking place on most that fall into the hands of the National Trust, as at Cotehele (Cornwall), and also on such privately owned ones as the dovecote at Rousham (Oxfordshire). Inside, the dovecote can be seen to contain hundreds of nesting holes set in rows and built into the brick or stone walls, sometimes extending from the eaves down to floor level. (At Athelhampton (Dorset) there are 1,000 holes). The entrance for the birds is somewhere in the roof, either a simple hole, dormers or on the surrounding cupola. The size varies probably with the wealth of the original owner—the older monastic and manorial dovecotes are splendid affairs.

Regional building materials and styles also vary; timber seems to be popular in the west country, stone in Dorset, Wiltshire, Oxfordshire, Northamptonshire and Warwickshire and brick in East Anglia. By no means are dovecotes exclusive to gardens, but there are several noteworthy ones in gardens open to the public, and frequently imposing dovecotes are nearby at the home farm or in the village.

At Rousham (Oxfordshire) the dovecote is comparatively small. It is round and is in an old-world corner of the garden amid rose beds with clipped box edging and a nearby mulberry tree. Not far away at Chastleton House (Oxfordshire) the dovecote is across the road from the garden, while at Nymans (Sussex) it is built into the wall and is surrounded by camelias, magnolias and rhododendrons. Notable examples are quite frequent and those at Kyre Park (Worcestershire), Compton Wynyates (Warwickshire) and Bingham's Melcombe (Dorset) are worth investigation.

Aviaries

The keeping of decorative birds such as black swans, Chinese geese, peacocks and guineafowl is a common practice of ancient association. The Chinese emperors commonly introduced exotic birds as decoration and life to their palace gardens. Aviaries, as such, are none too common though a particularly good example is to be seen at Waddesdon Manor (Buckinghamshire) where a formal rose garden is set apart to house a fantastic pavilion-like aviary. Statuary, fountain and ferns form the centre, flanked by well-maintained cages full of interesting birds. Colourful parrots have free range nearby and fly about in neighbouring horse chestnut trees. The aviary and its accompanying garden were in a serious state of disrepair after the war when the estate became the property of the National Trust. The garden was replanned on simple and pleasing lines, the lawn is bordered by white roses ('Iceberg') and a white pebble path.

The Chinese aviary at Dropmore (Buckinghamshire) stretches along the walk bordering the Queen's Walk (so called because when Queen Victoria used to visit Lord Grenville at Dropmore—sometimes, it is said, for breakfast—she had to pass along this path because there was no carriage drive to the house). This aviary at Dropmore no longer houses birds but is a remarkably magnificent iron structure in a Chinese style. The old Ravens Cage at Regents Park (London), designed by Decimus Burton in 1880, was a great attraction in its day but has been superseded by the mid-twentieth century design by Lord Snowdon for the present bird house. At Harewood House (Yorkshire) a bird garden is to be opened to the public in 1970 which will include a tropical bird house and two or three acres will be given over to free range decorative birds. At Sezincote (Gloucestershire) a small Indianesque aviary, in keeping with the architecture of the house, houses budgerigars. At the Stagsden Bird Gardens (Bedfordshire) where there are numberless species of birds to be seen, there is a garden of shrub roses containing quite a good selection as a supplementary attraction to the birds.

Statuary of varying quality is to be found in many gardens, sometimes unfortunately badly defaced by the weather or of little beauty under the grasp of ivy, or just in blatant poor taste. On the other hand excellent work can be seen in the equestrian statue of King John Sobieski of Poland at Newby Hall (Yorkshire) or the various figures of stone or lead at Rousham (Oxfordshire). In the garden there, across the bowling green from the house, is Scheemaker's *Lion attacking a Horse*. Scheemaker's work can also be found at Stowe (Buckinghamshire), Shrugborought (Staffordshire) and Chiswick Park (London) where he shares the setting with Rysbrack and where too the exedra houses vases and statues from Hadrian's villa near

Tivoli. The garden at **Anglesey Abbey** (Cambridgeshire) recently acquired by the National Trust and opened to the public, houses an extensive collection of statuary, motley in content but excellent in array and each piece enhanced by its location.

At **Iford Manor** (Wiltshire) Sir Harold Peto designed the terrace with colonnades to house statuary, some of it his own, and his garden is perhaps one of the best surviving examples of the use of stone and plants in the right proportions. At **Easton Neston** (Northamptonshire) the statuary is almost dwarfed by the scale of the formal garden. Statuary is also to be seen at **Wilton House** (Wiltshire) and **Hever Castle** (Kent) and more up-to-date examples like the work of Barbara Hepworth and Henry Moore are to be found in several of the Greater London Council parks and open spaces and in private gardens such as **Dartington Hall** (Devon) where Henry Moore's figure *Reclining Woman* is housed near the open air theatre. At the **Old Vicarage, Bucklebury** (Berkshire) a large figure by Henry Moore looks out over the surrounding countryside, but can be moved on its turntable, to look towards the garden.

Shrine of Worthies at Stowe, Buckinghamshire

Sundials in themselves would provide the subject of a book, but the garden visitor may derive much pleasure from 'collecting' sundials. Each one varies from the others, there is no standard of size or design and while many accurately record the time of day there are many more whose sole function is to provide interest and to emphasise the timelessness of Nature and gardens. An assortment of mottos and quotations accompany these time pieces, many classic examples of the fleeting nature of life and others pure 'God-wottery'. The horizontal type of sundial is usually used as a centre piece to a rose garden, formal garden or herb garden, while the vertical ones—some of them quite handsome—are fastened to the walls of buildings or gatehouses. Note the one on the library wall at Queen's College (Cambridge) painted in brilliant colours, depicting the signs of the zodiac, and another remarkable one in the garden of Merton College (Oxford). Two large stone sundials of the 'facet-headed' type or polyhedrons have recently been restored at Penshurst Place (Kent), one of seventeenth century origin and the other dating from the eighteenth century. The former is an elaborate one with 22 time-telling facets, so that in sunshine several facets may show the time simultaneously. These have been lying almost unnoticed at Penshurst until recently and have been installed for the public to see. Other sundials to note are at Nostell Priory (Yorkshire), Kiftsgate Court (Gloucestershire), a ten-faced sundial at Barrington Court (Somerset), Knowsley Hall (Lancashire), Kingston Lacey (Dorset), Clumber Park (Nottinghamshire), and Sudeley Castle (Gloucestershire) where the sundial is believed to be the original medieval one.

There are several attempts at making sundials of living material, the most successful at Ascott (Buckinghamshire) where the gnome is of yew with a decorative finial of golden yew grafted on to it. The Roman figures surrounding it are clipped in box and surrounding these is a motto in yew "Light and shade by turn but love always".

Ice Houses

The forerunner of the refrigerator, specially constructed in the garden, was the so-called ice house, where snow or ice could be kept in order to prolong the keeping of food. Ice was packed into the houses, which were all constructed either by excavating or by forming some deep grotto-like tunnel, cave or igloo-like structure in a bank. The remains of such, and some doubtful remains of others, are to be seen in some gardens. One of the best is at Tapeley Park (Devon).

THE LIVING ARCHITECTURE OF THE GARDEN

It is almost taken for granted that trees play an important role in the foundation of our landscape and an aspect without them in a garden is unthinkable. But, surprisingly, very few trees are native to this country and the visitor to any garden or park can always be assured of an exercise in recognition of trees. Their bark, general skeleton and buds give away their identity in winter, and their leaves and flowers in summer make naming them a far easier entertainment. The ash, beech, hawthorn, cherry, holly, hornbeam, some oaks, limes and elms are British; otherwise almost everything has been introduced and one might marvel at how well they have naturalised themselves.

There are two main types of trees: the evergreen which keep their leaves in winter, like the native holly, and the deciduous or leaf-loosing which reveal their bare framework in winter like the oaks and elms. Most of the evergreen trees we enjoy in our parks and gardens in winter are coniferous or cone bearing and have leaves like needles; the pines and firs are examples. Most of them were introduced into Britain from North America during the nineteenth century—and as they have grown the face of our landscape has changed. Sometimes only a few seeds were sent home, most of which went to Kew, and the rest to a few collectors. One such was Lord Grenville at Dropmore (Buckinghamshire). His **pinetum** (collection of conifers) was begun in the winter of 1795-6 and enlarged between 1830 and 1840 to extend round the lake. It is still one of the best collections in the country and has consistently been added to. Other such collections are to be seen at Eridge Castle (Sussex), Bicton Gardens (Devon) where there are notable specimens, the National Pinetum at Bedgebury (Kent), now the most representative collection in England, and Westonbirt (Gloucestershire). Many gardens have a minor pinetum, notably Wisley (Surrey) and Terling Place (Essex) and generally in pinetum the trees are labelled with their names. At Thrumpton Hall (Nottinghamshire) there is a collection of larches and cedars planted to commemorate historical events since the coronation of George III.

Deciduous trees have quite a different story. Since the middle ages the growing of trees near houses has represented wealth, custom, charm against evil spirits and (at its simplest) summer shade. 'Capability' Brown and Bridgeman started the fashion for planting deciduous trees informally and in groups or as salient features of a scheme. There are many gardens in which trees play a major role in the effect, no English garden exists without trees but some are noteworthy for either the variety of trees collected there or the size or age of the specimens. At Alderwood House (Berkshire) there are upwards of two hundred and fifty trees, all named, planted by A. Bruce Jackson of Kew, and at Hyde Crook (Dorset) is a collection of trees and shrubs made by William Bean of Kew. But visit also Polesden Lacey (Surrey), Holkham Hall (Norfolk), Wilton House (Wiltshire), Bramham Park (Yorkshire), Corby Castle (Cumberland), Leonardslea (Sussex), Hassop Hall (Derbyshire), Batsford Park (Gloucestershire), Lacock Abbey (Wiltshire), and, particularly in autumn, Sheffield Park (Sussex) for the autumn colour. At Ascott (Buckinghamshire) the collection has been made considering the contrast in leaf colour and there is interesting mixed planting to be seen there. This garden contains good yew hedges and some simple **topiary.** Generally, one associates topiary with formal Jacobean gardens such as are to be seen at Hatfield (Hertfordshire), Sudeley Castle (Gloucestershire), Levens Hall (Westmorland), Chilham Castle (Kent), but there are many isolated examples of trees and shrubs having been clipped into geometric shapes in gardens other than formal ones. That the practice of clipping plants in this way was carried on in Tudor times (and even before) in England is in no doubt, but the vogue increased when William and Mary came to the throne and the Dutch court brought over many of its customs. Dutch gardens as such can be seen at Westbury Court (Gloucestershire) and Sutton Place (Surrey), and at Kensington Palace (London).

Levens Hall (Westmorland) is one of the most famous topiary gardens in the world, and at present another part of the garden is threatened by plans for a local by-pass road. There is good topiary at Compton Wynyates (Warwickshire) and at Packwood House (Warwickshire) where the topiary garden is said to represent the Sermon on the Mount, the Master, the Twelve Apostles and the Multitude being clearly depicted. The topiary garden itself is a large rectangular plot enclosed on two sides by a yew hedge, and various-sized conical yews are said to represent the Multitude advancing towards the Mount. On the far side (from the house) of the rectangular garden, there is a pathway bordered by twelve yews, said to depict the Apostles, with four larger trees in their midst—the Evangelists. A spiral path enclosed by a hedge then leads up to the tree that is representative of Christ.

The scale of the shrubs subjected to this clipping varies and one can expect to see dark tall yews in ponderous form, or almost toy-like shapes at Haseley Court (Oxfordshire) where there is a remarkable topiary garden, open to the wide views to the Cotswolds beyond, and not encumbered by surrounding formality,. There is a new garden at Kew representative of a seventeenth century garden which can be explored. (For a full list of topiary gardens see *Discovering Topiary* in this series.)

The ever-attractive fascination of the miniature is indulged in some instances by such clipped hedges round flower beds, either in elaborate formal designs making patterns or merely as a decorative addition. In old kitchen gardens one can expect to see the remains of box edging used in this way—but it is a relic of the days when labour was cheap and a boy could always be spared to keep the box edges clipped squarely. Further evidence of the hours the gardeners had at their disposal can be confirmed in the fun that was provided for in the gardens. The planting and the making, over the years, of a **maze** must have provided the workers themselves with hours of work and much ingenuity in designing the 'garden'. Mazes can be seen still at Hampton Court (Middlesex) laid out probably about 1690, at Somerleyton Hall (Suffolk), Hever Castle (Kent) and Glendurgan (Cornwall). At Hatfield House (Hertfordshire) there is a recently-made reproduction of a maze.

The formal planting of trees in a row or in staggered row, can make either a screen or windbreak or, if a double line is put in, an **avenue,** frequently used to line a driveway or approach road as at Studley College (Warwickshire) where 35 wellingtonias line the drive, or the impressive Spanish chestnut avenue at Croft Castle (Herefordshire), the oldest avenue in the country probably planted at the time of the Restoration, or the oak avenue at Chillington Hall (Staffordshire), or of monkey puzzle trees at Bicton Garden (Devon), or tulip trees at Eridge Castle (Kent). The effect of repetition in the pattern formation produces some interesting results. At Clumber Park (Nottinghamshire) the avenue curves for three miles or so and is thought to be the longest in England. Visit Mapledurham House (Oxfordshire) supposedly the setting for *Wind in the Willows*—for thereabouts are the water wheel, the willows and reeds and, of course, the Thames. Restoration is in progress there and the old elm avenue has been replaced by young lime trees. Here too at each side of the porch is a magnolia claimed to be the oldest in England. The felling of trees to provide for a thoroughfare may not be such a present-day activity as we suppose. An avenue was cut at St. Paul's Waldenbury (Hertfordshire) through the woods and, flanked by a beech hedge, it rises along a grass path to the statue of Hercules. Not far away the great vista from the Bridgewater Monument to Ashridge House (Hertfordshire) has been cut through the beech woods. At Hidcote Manor (Gloucestershire) the effect of an avenue with the sky beyond is dramatically achieved by dark hollies and then elms arching over a wide grassy slope. At Levens Hall (Westmorland) the oak avenue planted at the end of the seventeenth century is at present threatened by road development for the proposed Kendal by-pass. This avenue was originally designed as an approach to the gardens by Beaumont.

When trees are planted in a row and the branches interlaced to form what at first appears to be a hedge on stilts, the trees are said to be **pleached.** Good examples are to be seen at Bateman's (Sussex) and Hidcote Manor (Gloucestershire), Sissinghurst Castle (Kent), where there is a pleached lime walk, and another at St. Paul's Waldenbury (Hertfordshire), Kensington Palace Garden (London) and Knebworth House (Hertfordshire). Pleaching is an ancient art in training trees, taking time to be effective as the young branches are interlaced with those of their neighbours. Wires are used to train the trees in this way and can be removed once the wood has hardened and the branches hold their shape. A short avenue of limes, comparatively recently planted and being trained in this way, can be studied in the water garden at Hemel Hempstead (Hertfordshire). The wires form a skeleton arcade at present, but one day the trees will fold over the walk providing shade and no doubt the plan is to put seats there for the enjoyment of the public.

Herb Gardens

There is probably more romantic twaddle written about herbs and herb gardens than any other group of plants! Up to the seventeenth century the application of medicine was not scientific but was bound by plant lore and superstition. The monastery gardens were, undoubtedly, the earliest herb gardens, where in the infirmary garden a stock of plants, traditionally used for healing, was grown. It has been the prerogative of the mistress of the house to grow and provide herbs for both medicinal and culinary use for the past 400 years, since the dissolution of the monastries; and while many simple herb collections exist in kitchen gardens and cottage gardens there are a few noteworthy ones, worth a visit from the interested enthusiast. Understandably, such plants have played a considerable role in the lives of our forefathers not only as flavouring for feed and benison in distress but as tokens and decorations at festivals. The close connection between pharmacy and botany was inevitable, dovetailing in many instances in the past and the herbalist/barber-surgeon/apothecary became a figure of considerable importance. The bibliophile can start at this point the discovery of botanical and gardening literature, for from the early seventeenth century Gerarde and Parkinson were working in London and publishing their *Herbals* and gardening in what is now the City of London and the heart of Covent Garden Market, respectively. Hundreds of books have been published on plants. Many of them have charming illustrations, hand coloured and drawn from life and are to be seen in private collections as well as in such libraries as at The Royal Botanic Garden, Kew, The Lindley Library, London, The Linnaean Society's Library, London, The Natural History Museum, London, The Bodleian Library, Oxford and many city and municipal libraries. The early "physic gardens" were started as collections of plants of scientific value but soon became botanic gardens as such. The Oxford Botanic Garden was the first to be founded in 1621, and the Chelsea Physic Garden next on its present site in 1673. (Unfortunately this interesting garden is not open to the public). The Royal Botanic Garden, Kew was originally the Kew Physic Garden (1760) and still contains a very interesting herb garden, with the plants clearly labelled. At the Royal Horticultural Society's Gardens, Wisley (Surrey), a good representative collection of herbs is to be found at the top of the rock garden towards the Alpine House. At Knole (Kent) the herb garden has a circular central bed with spokes of santolina radiating from it, each segment of a wheel thus formed is filled with coloured foliage herbs such as red sage, and golden marjoram. Beautifully secluded so that the aroma of the herbs can be savoured, is the herb garden at Sissinghurst Castle (Kent). Here some of the decorative artemesias and rosemary add lightness to the effect and look splendid against the surrounding yew hedges.

One of the most interesting features at Hardwick Hall (Derbyshire) is a herb walk that has been added quite recently. The long beds which border a central path are planted up with a collection in excess of a hundred different kinds of herb. Many plants here will be recognised as border plants, or only known as inhabitants of the decorative parts of the garden, so comprehensive is the collection; but they are included quite legitimately.

A recently constructed herb garden, planned along the simplest lines, can be seen at the end of the South Terrace at the American Museum, Claverton Manor (Somerset). A beehive forms the central point in an otherwise simple formal but quite comprehensive garden. An interesting garden, otherwise, Claverton Manor provides examples in scale planning especially of the terraces, and there is also a reconstruction of part of George Washington's eighteenth century garden at Mount Vernon, Virginia, U.S.A. Clipped box and a peacock in topiary adorn a pleasant little herb garden at the Old Vicarage, Bucklebury (Berkshire). Many small private gardens boast a herb border, albeit part of the general potager—some of them form interesting collections. Herbs have been included in the roof garden at the new College of Food and Domestic Arts, Birmingham.

The Living Elements

The plant material that goes to colour the palette of each garden is selected and has always been someone's personal choice. The ways in which it is used—for effect, for detail, for screening, clothing walls or pillars, to provide shade and shelter—are what goes to make each garden unique. The acquisition of knowledge of plants can take many forms (and indeed many years) but the use of the right plant for the right purpose is something the garden visitor of the most amateur outlook can easily learn to recognise. Trees break up the landscape, screen, shelter or set the stage. Shrubs are usually massed either exclusively or are underplanted with bulbs or interplanted with perennials. Flowering and foliage-effect perennials are the permanent residents of the herbaceous border and such schemes, while annuals, like marigolds, nasturtiums and petunias, are used to provide a quick gay summer effect. England is justly famous for her lawns, time and money is afforded for them out of proportion to other aspects of gardening—but it cannot be denied that a well-groomed lawn sets off the rest of the garden to perfection. It is our inclement climate that makes our gardens possible, and England is rich not only in her stately homes and their encircling gardens and parks but in the ability of the Englishman to put to use the wealth of plant material available to him.

Iris Hardwick
1. *A garden pavilion and fountains in Kensington Gardens, London.*
2. *The sweeping landscape and Palladian Bridge at Prior Park, Bath.*
Iris Hardwick

Iris Hardwick
3. Henry Moore's *Reclining Woman* at Dartington Hall, Devon.

4. *A flight of brick steps at Chilham Castle, Kent.*

Peter Hunt

5. Peto's Colonnade Terrace at Iford Manor, Wiltshire.

Iris Hardwick

Iris Hardwick

6. *The stage, with wings, of the open air theatre at Dartington Hall, Devon.*
7. *Hyde Park, London, is a popular recreational centre besides being a lovely garden.*

Ruth Rutter

Iris Hardwick
8. *The Yew Garden, designed by Sir Edwin Lutyens, at Ammerdown Park near Bath, Somerset.*
9. *The boundary wall of the old courtyard garden, with gazebo and balustrading, at Montacute, Somerset.*
Iris Hardwick

Iris Hardwick

10. The orangery at Saltram House, Devon, designed by Robert Adam and recently restored.

Peter Hunt

11. Orange trees in traditional tubs at Saltram House, Devon.

Iris Hardwick

12. The gatehouse and bronze urn at Lanhydrock, Cornwall.

Peter Hunt

13. At Hodnet Hall, Shropshire, the informal water is bordered by primulas and other bog-loving plants.

Kay N. Sanecki
14. The cloister in the Monk's Garden at Ashridge, Hertfordshire.

Peter Hunt

15. In the National Pinetum, Bedgebury, Kent.

Iris Hardwick

16. A fountain provides movement at Bicton Gardens, Devon.

Iris Hardwick

17. Terracing with balustrades overlooking the Italian topiary garden at Lindridge Park, Devon.

18. Small gardens are sometimes 'prefabricated' as at The Bear Hotel, Marlborough, Wiltshire.

Iris Hardwick

Iris Hardwick

19. *The Italian Garden at Compton Acres, Dorset, now a public park.*

20. *The ice house at Tapeley Park, Instow, Devon.*

Iris Hardwick

Iris Hardwick

21. *Garden house and pond garden at Tintinhull, Somerset.*

Peter Hunt

22. *Walls shelter the formal pool and statuary at Sledmere, Yorkshire.*

23. The formal clipped hedges at Sissinghurst Castle, Kent, enclose a series of gardens when seen from the tower.

Peter Hunt

24. Elaborate topiary at Compton Wynyates, a Tudor house in Warwickshire.

Iris Hardwick

25. *A formal treatment of statuary, topiary and trees at Belton House, Lincolnshire.*

Peter Hunt

26. *The simplicity of the pool at Knightshayes Court, Devon, is dramatic.*

Iris Hardwick

27. *The iron work aviary at Dropmore, Buckinghamshire*

Peter Hunt

Peter Hunt

28. *Small lily-pool and figure at Burton Agnes, Yorkshire.*

29. *The large dovecote at Athelhampton, Dorset.*

Iris Hardwick

GLOSSARY

Arboretum: a collection of trees, both evergreen and deciduous.

Bedding: close planting in formal manner to make patterns or colour combinations of plants raised elsewhere. Seen most commonly in public parks and municipal gardens during the summer.

Carpet Bedding: the employment of small plants usually with coloured foliage for bedding (q.v.) Calendars, mottos, etc. are constructed in this way in municipal gardens.

Chinoiserie: the name given to a style fashionable during the whole of the eighteenth century—a counterfeit form of Chinese taste. The pagoda at Kew is an example.

Dutch Garden: a formal style of garden, incorporating clipped plants on geometric lines and enclosed water.

Elizabethan Garden: a formal style evolved in the time of Elizabeth I, with terraces, walks, topiary, sweet smelling plants which were at the time first being grown in gardens, arbours, heraldic statuary, etc.

Formal Garden: a site in which some symmetry of design is detectable, be it elaborate as in a parterre or simple as in a rectangular lily pool. Often a formal garden is constructed upon a level site or a series of level sites incorporating terraces, steps and walling.

French Gardening: a system of intensive cultivation of fruit and vegetables. The use of cloches, frames, close intercropping and the training of fruit trees to produce heavier crops in less space.

French-style Gardens: elaborate layouts rigid in conception influenced by French taste in the seventeenth century. Melbourne Hall (Derbyshire), though changed, provides a basic example.

Gazebo: a small building, usually of two storeys, set at some vantage point in the garden for watching the approaches or the surrounding countryside.

Grotto: an eighteenth century foible, grotto making resulted in a collection of stones to form 'houses' and 'caves' and 'tunnels'. Frequently the resultant buildings were lined with shells, bones, fossils, or attractive pebbles.

Ha Ha: a ditch, invisible from the garden, constructed to prevent entry and thus avoiding the building of a fence which would impair the view. In section it is a ditch with one side upright (estate side) and the other side sloping (common land side).

Informal Garden: a plan devoid of formality or straight lines. A garden designed to look natural, like a woodland garden (q.v.) or beds of plants set about in a seemingly haphazard manner.

Italianate Garden: a garden designed along the lines of the Italian style. i.e. terraces, balustrades, stairways, elaborate fountains, ornate statuary all within formal lines.

Jacobean Garden: the formal stylised designs beloved in the seventeenth century. Topiary, formal planting, high clipped hedges, herb gardens, knots, etc.

Parterre: a symmetrical, formally designed garden of considerable proportion intended to be looked upon from above so that the whole pattern could be viewed.

Pergola: a structure for the support of climbing plants. Most frequently seen as a continuous archway over a pathway, but also to be found as a screen and patio cover.

Pinetum: a collection of conifers, or cone bearing trees.

Physic Garden: a forerunner of the botanic garden, for specialised interest in medicinal plants.

Rustic Work: the employment of barked wood in forming trellises, pergolas, summer houses, seats, etc., usually comparatively short-lived structures. The style is sometimes copied in cast iron especially for the fashioning of seats.

Sunken Garden: an area, usually small, constructed at a lower level than the surrounding garden. Planted in a formal manner, it creates a design to be seen as a whole, or a picture to be looked upon.

Terrace: a raised level space, in garden architecture usually running along a wall of a house or the retaining wall of a higher terrace. Terracing is a method of traversing a steeply sloping site. Many instances exist of the terrace forming the transitional link between house and garden.

Topiary: the practice of clipping evergreens into geometrical and other forms.

Trellage: an elaborate trellis, with some additional and non-functional ornament.

Water Garden: a garden in which water is featured in either formal or informal confines or as fountains, cascades or spouts.

Wild Garden: an informal planting of trees and shrubs with under-planting of shade loving plants and bulbs often naturalised.

Woodland Garden: a plantation of trees and shrubs emulating woodland, sometimes as a wild garden (q.v.) or a shrub collection as in rhododendron gardens, beneath existing trees.

GARDENS WITH SPECIAL FEATURES

These lists are not exhaustive, by any means; but are intended as a guide to the garden visitor with special interests.

Formal Gardens

Innumerable gardens are laid out on formal lines; some achieve good effect, others are an eyesore; the gardens listed below are probably the best known examples.

Anglesey Abbey (Cambridgeshire)
Bicton Gardens (Devon)
Blenheim Palace (Oxfordshire)
Blickling (Norfolk)
Bramham Park (Yorkshire)
Buscot Park (Berkshire)
Castle Ashby (Northamptonshire)
Chatsworth (Derbyshire)
Compton Wynyates (Warwickshire)
Cothay Manor (Somerset)
Easton Neston (Northamptonshire)
Gunby Hall (Lincolnshire)
Hampton Court (Middlesex)
Hascombe Court (Surrey)
Hatfield House (Hertfordshire)
Hidcote Manor (Gloucestershire)
Holkham Hall (Norfolk)
Knightshayes Court (Devon)
Lanhydrock (Cornwall)
Lyegrove (Gloucestershire)
Melbourne Hall (Derbyshire)
Montacute (Somerset)
Oxburgh Hall (Norfolk)
Packwood House (Warwickshire)
Shrubland Park (Suffolk)
Sissinghurst (Kent) a series of gardens
Sudeley Castle (Gloucestershire)
Waddesdon (Buckinghamshire)
Westbury Court (Gloucestershire)
Wilton House (Wiltshire)

Informal Gardens

All woodland and shrub gardens are informal gardens, and many examples are to be found of parkland surrounding a more formal treatment near the house.

Alton Towers (Staffordshire)
Biddulph Grange (Staffordshire)
Bressingham Hall (Norfolk)
Cotehele (Cornwall)
East Lambrook Manor (Somerset)
Harlow Car (Yorkshire)

Hodnet Hall (Shropshire)	Sheffield Park (Sussex)
Kettering Hall (Norfolk)	Stourhead (Wiltshire)
Killerton (Devon)	Stowe (Buckinghamshire)
Lee Ford (Devon)	Tresco Abbey (Isles of Scilly)
Leonardslea (Sussex)	University Botanic Garden Birmingham
Muncaster Castle (Cumberland)	
Rousham (Oxfordshire)	Wisley (Surrey)
Savill Gardens (Berkshire)	

Gardens in which water is of particular interest

Ammerdown	(Somerset)
Arden Croft	(Warwickshire)
Ascott	(Buckinghamshire) Fountains & lily pool.
Athelhampton	(Dorset)
Blagrave Hall	(Leicestershire)
Blenheim Palace	(Oxfordshire) Italian water garden and lake made by 'Capability' Brown.
Bohunt Manor	(Hampshire)
Bramham Park	(Yorkshire)
Brooksbury Agricultural College	(Leicestershire)
Buckhurst Park	(Berkshire) Waterfalls, cascades, etc.
Burgrove Hall	(Shropshire)
Buscot Park	(Berkshire)
Chartwell	(Kent) Lake with black swans and water garden.
Chilham Castle	(Kent)
Creech Grange	(Dorset) Cascades
Duxford Mill	(Cambridgeshire) Old water mill and miller's house, recorded in Domesday Book.
Easton Neston	(Northamptonshire)
Forde Abbey	(Somerset) Old moat and swan pool.
Furneaux Pelham Hall	(Hertfordshire)
Gunby Hall	(Lincolnshire) Moat garden.
Heaselands	(Sussex)
Hever Castle	(Kent) Moat and 35 acre-lake.
Hodnet Hall	(Shropshire) Informal lakes.
Holkham Hall	(Norfolk)
Knights Hall	(Berkshire) Bog and water garden.
Ludstone Hall	(Shropshire) Moated Jacobean house with former moat and fish ponds.
Netherscale Old Hall	(Staffordshire)

New Hall	(Warwickshire)
Nostell Priory	(Yorkshire) Boating on the lake.
Orchardleigh Park	(Somerset) Thirteenth century church on an island at the edge of the lake.
Pusey House	(Berkshire) Lake with white 'Chinese' bridge.
St. Paul's Waldenbury	(Hertfordshire)
Scotney Castle	(Kent) Moat and ruined castle.
Sezincote	(Gloucestershire) Indian water garden.
Sheffield Park	(Sussex) Informal lakes, best in autumn when colourful trees are reflected.
Sparsholt Park	(Berkshire) Parts of the water garden still in preparation.
Stourhead	(Wiltshire) Lake.
Studley Royal	(Yorkshire)
Tebworth Hall	(Bedfordshire)
The Mill House	(Hampshire)
Trebatha	(Cornwall) Swan pool and cascades.
Trentham Park	(Cheshire)
Waddesdon	(Buckinghamshire) Formal fountains.
Westbury Court	(Gloucestershire) Formal Dutch water garden.
Whelford Mill	(Gloucestershire) Mill and pool.
Wisley	(Surrey) Rock and water garden and lake.
Wrest Park	(Bedfordshire) Formal fountains and canal.

Gardens where either walls and wall shrubs or walled gardens can be seen

Alderley Grange	(Gloucestershire) New wall.
Alton Towers	(Staffordshire) Scallop-top wall.
Athelhampton	(Dorset)
Babworth Park	(Kent)
Brizes Park	(Essex)
Bury St. Edmunds Abbey	(Essex) Serpentine wall behind the rose border.
Charney Manor	(Berkshire)
Chartwell	(Kent) Wall built by Sir Winston Churchill.
Cotehele	(Cornwall)
Croft Castle	(Herefordshire) Walled garden.
Easton Neston	(Northamptonshire)
Fawnlees Hall	(Yorkshire)
Foston Old Rectory	(Co. Durham)

Friar's Gate   (Sussex)
Glemham   (Suffolk) Wall of red brick.
Haddon Hall   (Derbyshire)
Hever Castle   (Kent)
Hexton Manor   (Hampshire)
Houghton Lodge   (Hampshire)
Julians   (Hertfordshire)
Kelvedon Hall   (Essex) Walled rose garden.
Lacock Abbey   (Wiltshire)
Lazonby   (Cumberland)
Montacute   (Somerset) Walls with Elizabethan gazebos.
Nymans   (Sussex) Walls of old burnt-out house, plants survived.
Oxford Botanic Garden   (Oxfordshire)
Packwood   (Warwickshire) Walls with old cavity heating, and bee boles.
Raby Castle   (Co. Durham) Large walled formal garden.
St. Nicholas   (Yorkshire)
Stanhope Hall   (Norfolk)
The Deanery, Sonning   (Oxfordshire) The walled garden is all that remains of the Palace of Salisbury, from the See of Wessex.
Theydon Priory   (Essex)
Thorpe Hall   (Lincolnshire)
Walcott Hall   (Shropshire) Wall with gazebo. House was the home of Clive of India.
Wallington Gardens   (Northumberland) Kitchen garden now a walled pleasure garden.
Wrest Park   (Bedfordshire)

Gardens with dovecotes

Athelhampton (Dorset)
Bingham's Melcombe (Dorset)
Charleston Manor (Sussex)
Compton Wynyates (Warwickshire)
Cotehele (Cornwall)
Daglingworth (Gloucestershire)
Holcombe Court (Devonshire)
Holywell Hall (Rutlandshire)
Kyre Park (Worcestershire)
Naunton (Gloucestershire)
Nymans (Sussex)
Old Sufton (Herefordshire)
Quenington (Gloucestershire)
Rousham (Oxfordshire)
Snowshill Manor (Gloucestershire)
The White House (Shropshire)

Gardens with aviaries

Brackenber Lodge (Surrey)
Coverwood (Surrey)
Dropmore (Buckinghamshire)
    No birds.
Glynde Place (Sussex)
Gun Hill Place (Essex)
Heaselands (Sussex)
Knole (Kent)
    Exotic bird house
Mowton Cottage (Suffolk)
Sezincote (Gloucestershire)
The Glebe House
    (Northamptonshire)
Three Gates House
    (Warwickshire)
Tong (Shropshire)
    Egyptian hen house
Waddesdon
    (Buckinghamshire)
    One of the best aviaries.

Gardens of botanical interest

Beaumont Hall
    (University of Leicester)
Borde Hill (Sussex)
Bressingham Hall (Norfolk)
Corsham Court (Wiltshire)
Digberry (Oxfordshire)
Earnley Place (Sussex)
East Lambrook Manor
    (Somerset)
Great Dixter (Sussex)
Grey Court
    (Northamptonshire)
Harlow Car (Yorkshire)
Hidcote (Gloucestershire)
High Down (Sussex)
High Hackhurst (Surrey)
Iford Manor (Wiltshire)
Lacock Abbey (Wiltshire)
Newby Hall (Yorkshire)
Northbourne Court (Kent)
Nymans (Sussex)
Royal Botanic Gardens, Kew
    (Surrey)
St. Nicholas (Yorkshire)
Savill Garden (Berkshire)
Sewerby Hall (Yorkshire)
Sissinghurst Castle (Kent)
Thorpe Perrow (Yorkshire)
Tresco Abbey (Isles of Scilly)
Underway (Somerset)
University Botanic Garden
    (Birmingham)
University Botanic Garden
    (Bristol)
University Botanic Garden
    (Cambridge)
University Botanic Garden
    (Liverpool) at Ness, Wirrall
University Botanic Garden
    (Oxford)
Waterperry (Oxfordshire)
Wisley (Surrey)
Withersdane Hall
    (Wye College, Kent)
Yielding Tree
    (Worcestershire)

Herb gardens

Alderley Grange (Gloucestershire)
Claverton Manor (Somerset) American Museum
Hardwick Hall (Derbyshire)
Hertfordshire House (Buckinghamshire)

Knole **(Kent)**
Lullingstone Castle (Kent) Designed by Eleanor Sinclair
 Rhode, but replanted since.
Plantation House (Isle of Ely)
Scotney Castle (Kent)
The Old Vicarage Bucklebury (Berkshire)
and at most Botanic Gardens.

Gardens in which trees are a special feature

Trees form a part of every garden, and this list is by no means exhaustive, but offers some suggestions.
Indicates an arboretum.

Aldbury Park (Surrey) Trees planted by John Evelyn.
Alderwood House (Berkshire) Trees planted by A. Bruce Jackson of Kew.
Antony House (Cornwall) Famous *Ginko bilboa,* and large cone-shaped yew house.
Ammerdown Park (Somerset)
Ascott (Buckinghamshire) Colour planting of trees.
Audley End (Essex)
Batsford Park* (Gloucestershire)
Bedgbury* (Sussex) National Pinetum.
Bicton Gardens (Devon)
Borde Hill (Sussex)
Bramham Park (Yorkshire)
Chiswick Park (London) Cedars.
Clare College (Cambridgeshire) Metasequoia.
Corsham Court (Wiltshire) Tulip trees.
Dartington Hall (Devon)
Deene Park (Northamptonshire)
Dillington House (Somerset)
Dropmore (Buckinghamshire)
Eastnor Castle (Herefordshire)
Easton Neston (Northamptonshire)
Fanhams Hall (Hertfordshire)
Glendurgan (Cornwall)
Grayswood Hill (Surrey)
Highclere Castle (Hampshire)
Holkham Hall (Norfolk)
Hyde Crook (Dorset) Laid out by Bean of Kew.
Hyde Park (London)
Jermyns House (Hampshire)
Kensington Gardens (London)

Killerton	(Devon) Old holm oaks, probably the largest in the country. Tulip trees.
Knightshayes Court	(Devon)
Lacock Abbey	(Wiltshire)
Leonardslea	(Sussex)
Longleat	(Wiltshire)
Minterne	(Dorset)
Newstead Abbey	(Nottinghamshire)
Pampisford Hall	(Cambridgeshire)
Peckover House	(Cambridgeshire)
Petworth House	(Sussex)
Polesden Lacey	(Surrey)
Powderham Castle	(Devon)
Redisham Hall	(Suffolk)
Royal Botanic Gardens, Kew	(Surrey)
St. Roches Arboretum*	(Sussex)
Sandown Hall	(Staffordshire)
Sheffield Park	(Sussex)
Somerleyton Hall	(Suffolk)
Syon Park	(Middlesex) The Gardening Centre.
Terling Place	(Essex) Conifers.
Tew Park	(Oxford) Some trees thereabouts planted by John C. Loudon.
Thrumpton Hall	(Nottinghamshire)
Westonbirt*	(Gloucestershire) School garden and arboretum.
Weston Park	(Shropshire)
Wilton House	(Wiltshire)
Winkworth*	(Surrey)
Woburn Abbey	(Bedfordshire)

Gardens with literary associations

Batemans	(Sussex) Home of Rudyard Kipling.
Compton Beauchamp	(Berkshire) The moated grange of *Tom Brown's Schooldays*.
Duxford Mill	(Cambridgeshire) Charles Kingsley reputed to have written part of *The Water Babies* while staying with the miller.
Field Place	(Sussex) Shelley's birthplace.
Godmersham Park	(Kent) Frequently visited by Jane Austin.

Hoddington House	(Hampshire) Home of Henry Fielding.
Mapledurham	(Berkshire) Visited frequently by Pope; supposedly the setting for *Wind in the Willows*.
Newstead Abbey	(Nottinghamshire) Byron relics.
Nuneham	(Oxfordshire) Goldsmith's *Deserted Village*.
Polesden Lacey	(Surrey) R. B. Sheridan spent time there and a walk in the garden bears his name.
Sissinghurst Castle	(Kent) Planted by Victoria Sackville West.
Somersby Rectory	(Lincolnshire) Tennyson's birthplace; he lived there until 1837 and wrote there *Lady of Shalot, The Lotus Eaters, Miranda in the Moated Grange, The May Queen, Morte d'Arthur*, and a large part of *In Memoriam*.
Waterston Manor	(Dorset) Featured in *Far from the Madding Crowd* by Thomas Hardy, as Weatherby.

SOME GARDENS TO VISIT

(N.T.) Belonging to the National Trust.
* Gardens with arboretum.

Most of the gardens listed are open regularly, others only occasionally; information should be sought in such publications as:

Historic Houses, Castles and Gardens in Great Britain and Ireland. An Index Publication (Published annually)
Gardens of England and Wales open to the Public under the National Gardens Scheme (Published annually).
Gardens to Visit The Gardeners' Sunday Organisation (Published annually).
Britain's Heritage The Automobile Association.
and in local papers, particularly at holiday times.

Many travel agents, particularly in the big cities, can give information about organised tours to visit gardens. The tours can be a day's outing or take several days. Many private societies and horticultural clubs have interesting summer programmes of garden visits; and are sometimes able to see gardens not generally open to the public. Public libraries, town halls and social centres are all likely places in which the would-be garden visitor may find information and plan his outings.

Bedfordshire

Luton Hoo, Luton	Rose garden rock and water garden, temple.
Woburn Abbey, Woburn	3,000 acre park and nature reserve. Trees, animals, zoo—to suit all tastes.
Wrest Park, Silsoe	Formal garden, water, roses, level site.

Berkshire

Alderwood House, nr. Newbury	Trees.
Buckhurst Park, Sunninghill	Water gardens, woodland, fowl.
Buscot Park, Faringdon	Formal garden designed by Peto.
Compton Beauchamp, Shrivenham	Moat, woodland.
Culham Court, Henley	Terraced garden. Good alpines.
Folly Farm, Sulhamstead	Garden designed by Sir Edwin Lutyens and Gertrude Jekyll. Azaleas and rhododendrons are a modern addition.
Frogmore Gardens, Windsor Castle	Royal mausoleum. Eighteenth century garden.
Manor Cottage, Sutton Courtney	Botanical interest.
Pusey House, Faringdon	Lake, shrubs, herbaceous plants, roses.
Savill Gardens, Windsor Great Park	Informal, botanical interest, large scale planting. Excellent for rhododendrons and azaleas and associated planting.
The Deanery, Sonning	Garden designed by Sir Edwin Lutyens. Old walls.

Buckinghamshire

Ascott, Wing	Terraced garden, good trees, water, view over Ivinghoe beacon. (N.T.)
Cliveden, Taplow	Terraces, informal planting and formal gardens recently neglected, but being renovated. (N.T.)
Dropmore, Taplow*	Pinetum, lake, aviary, chinoiserie.
Hertfordshire House, Coleshill	Medium sized garden, terraced lawns, trees, herb gardens.
Luxmoor's Garden, Eton College	On an island in the Thames, interesting plants. Nearby also the Provost's Garden and Fellows' Garden.

Stowe, Buckingham	Eighteenth century landscape garden, being renovated. Temples, lake, palladian bridge, trees. (Part N.T.)
Waddesdon Manor, Waddesdon	Formal garden, fountains, aviary, trees. (N.T.)

Cambridgeshire

Anglesey Abbey, Cambridge	Statuary, formal garden, trees. (N.T.)
Cambridge gardens	College gardens and University Botanic Garden. Recently completed rock garden in the Botanic Garden is one of the best in the country. The Fellows' Garden, Trinity College is superb in early spring. Garden of Clare College for trees, scented flowers and colour effect.
Duxford Mill, Cambridge	Small garden, but of interest.

Cheshire

Arley Hall, Northwich	Topiary, herbaceous borders.
Ashton Heys, Ashton	Woodland garden, flowering trees, rhododendrons, camellias and heathers.
Eaton Hall, Chester	Large formal garden, lakes, rhododendrons, flowering trees and shrubs.
Lyme Park, Disley	Enormous park, formal Dutch garden. (N.T.)
The Quarry, Prenton	Once a worked-out quarry, alpines, azaleas, rhododendrons.
Tatton Park, Knutsford	Garden buildings, lake, Repton design.

Cornwall

Antony House, Torpoint	Fine yew hedges and yew 'tree house'. (N.T.)
Caerhays Castle, Caerhays	Magnolias and rhododendrons.
Copeland Court, Truro	Former residence of the Bishops of Truro. Shrubs, trees.
Cotehele, Calstock	Informal planting, many tender plants, medieval dovecote, pretty pond and stream forming water garden. (N.T.)
Glendurgan Gardens, Helford	Trees and shrubs and a maze. (N.T.)
Lanhydrock House, Bodmin	Sycamore avenue and interesting gate house. Formal gardens with ornaments. (N.T.)

Hassop Hall*, Bakewell	Woodland garden, with arboretum in which is a collection unusual for the north.
Kedleston Hall, Derby	Serpentine lake, orangery.
Lea Rhododendron Gardens, Matlock	Woodland planting of rhododendrons collection and azaleas.
Melbourne Hall, Melbourne	Large formal garden designed in the eighteenth century, statuary, topiary, clipped yew tunnel and birdcage arbour of wrought iron.

Devon

Bicton Gardens*, East Budleigh	Large Italian garden, formal avenue of monkey puzzle trees, orangeries, pinetum and garden of North American shrubs. Palm house, conservatories and cacti house. All plants labelled.
Castle Drogo, Exeter	The last of the stately homes to be built. Garden designed by Sir Edwin Lutyens. Rose garden, herbaceous borders and wild garden.
Dartington Hall, Totnes	Large modernised garden, surrounding old house which is now used as a cultural centre for the arts. Grass open air theatre, modern statuary, bulbs, fine trees including outstanding Irish yews.
Killerton, Broad Clyst	Large formal, old garden gradually brought up to date by successive owners. Good trees and shrubs. (N.T.)
Knightshayes Court, Tiverton	Striking formal water garden very simple in its conception. Elsewhere, alpines and unusual plants, rhododendrons in spring.
Lee Ford, Budleigh Salterton	Bulbs, rhododendrons, magnolias in the spring, herbaceous plants in summer. Adam pavilion.
Luscombe Castle, Dawlish	Nineteenth century castle designed by Nash surrounded by Repton gardens. Good trees and shrubs, herbaceous plants.
Slade, Cornwood	Shrubs, walled garden, good pleached hornbeam alley.
Sharpham House, Ashprington	Numerous fine old and large trees, woodland garden with river, herbaceous borders.

Stonelands, Dawlish	Large informal garden with flowering trees and shrubs. Woodland and river side walks, lawns and heather garden.
Tapeley Park, Instow	Large terraced Italianate garden with statuary, formal hedges, sub-tropical plants.
The Garden House, Buckland	Terraced garden with good collection of flowering shrubs.

Dorset

Abbotsbury Sub-tropical Gardens, Abbotsbury	(Close to the swannery). Sub-tropical plants grow at the shore's edge, remarkable for magnolias and tender plants.
Athelhampton, Puddletown	Ten acres of formal and landscaped gardens, large dovecote, walled garden, herbaceous borders, good stone work and interesting gateway.
Colliston House, Poole	Collection of plants of botanical interest. Fine views over Poole Harbour and the Purbeck Hills.
Compton Acres, Poole	Seven separate gardens in varying styles; water garden, Japanese garden, Italian garden, Roman garden, rock garden, heath garden and tropical garden. Colour all the year round, valuable statuary and garden ornament.
Cranborne Manor, Wimborne	Good roses and rose species. Herbs, shrubs. Several enclosed gardens. Old loggia.
Forde Abbey, Chard	Old Cistercian Abbey, swans, eighteenth century long-pond, moat garden. Good collection of trees and shrubs; herbaceous material used well.
Hyde Crook, Dorchester	Orchid house, spring flowering trees and shrubs. (Only open March, April and May.)
Lulworth Manor, Lulworth	Worthwhile collection of shrubs, and walled garden of Lulworth Castle.
Minterne, Cerne Abbas	**Exceptional collection of rhododendrons and flowering shrubs. Beech trees of good age.**
St. Giles House, Wimborne St. Giles	Spacious garden, with eighteenth century shell grotto.
Yaffle Hill, Poole	Contemporary garden, heath planting and conifers.

Co. Durham

Auckland Castle, Auckland	Large park-garden, with sweeping lawns, greenhouses and kitchen garden.
Egglestone Hall, Egglestone	Spring bulbs, herbaceous borders and roses in summer, good lawns. Large gardens.
Headlam Hall, Gainford	Yew and beech hedges, herbaceous borders, stream and rose garden.
Neasham Abbey, Neasham	Good trees, and flowering trees and shrubs. Large rock garden, botanically interesting garden.
Quarriston, Heighington	Rhododendrons, meconopsis. Good views over the Tees valley.
Raby Castle, Nr. Darlington	Large walled garden with greenhouses, herbaceous borders, usually good sweet peas, old walnut trees.

Essex

Audley End House, Saffron Walden	Landscape is the work of 'Capability' Brown who widened the river Cam to form the lake. Temples.
Colne Ford House, Earls Colne	Flowering trees and shrubs, bulbs, old mulberry tree, tulip trees and medlar.
Colne Place, Earls Colne	Garden sheltered by 17ft. high clipped yew and holly hedge. Lilies, herbaceous plants and good colour.
Gun Hill Place, Dedham	Aviary, lake, good trees, Very attractive in spring when the bulbs and rhododendrons are in flower.
Hill Pasture, Broxted	Irises, shrubs and trees, bulbs in spring, water garden.
Kelvedon Hall, Brentwood	Lily pond, good yew hedges, walled rose garden of some importance. Considered colour planting.
St. Osyth's Priory, Clacton	Interesting flower gardens, trees and gatehouse.
Terling Place, Terling	Formal garden with clipped yews, roses and conifers.
Theydon Priory, Theydon Bois	Walled garden, bulbs in spring.

Gloucestershire

Abbotswood, Stow-in-the-Wold	In the heart of the Cotswolds, this modern garden offers much to be seen. Heather and rock garden slope behind the house, with water, shrubs herbaceous plants and alpines. Horticulturally interesting.

Alderley Grange, Alderley	Good old trees, contemporary walled garden and herb garden.
Barnsley House, Cirencester	Herbaceous borders and shrubs recently planted. Laburnum walk, and eighteenth century summer houses.
Batsford Park*, Moreton-in-the-Marsh	Trees, considerable eastern influence. Everything labelled.
Berkeley Castle, Berkeley	Walls of the castle effectively planted. Lily pond surrounded by yews.
Hidcote Manor Gardens, Chipping Campden	A series of gardens of varying types and yet united as a whole. Good hedges, pleaching and trees. Many interesting plants.
Kiftsgate Court, Chipping Campden	Roses. House clothed with roses and terraces attractively planted with old roses. A walk through *Rosa mundi* to a drop down the hillside to the bathing pool garden.
Lyegrove, Badminton	Botanically interesting. Formal garden, walls of Cotswold stone.
Melksham Court, Stinchcombe	Terraces, hedges and topiary, water garden, bulbs in spring, many interesting recently planted shrubs.
St. Francis, Lammas Park, Minchinhampton	Beech avenue, terraces, trough garden, herbaceous material. Recently made.
Sezincote, Moreton-in-the-Marsh	Indianesque garden, formal around house. Remarkable rock garden designed by Repton. Aviary. Conservatory corridors. Trees.
Sudeley Castle, Winchcombe	Formal gardens, topiary and medieval style hedges.
Westonbirt*, Tetbury	Arboretum, with superb colour effect all the year round. Conifers of perfect form and broadleaved trees of much interest.
Westonbirt School, Tetbury	Italianate terraces, fountains, remarkable trees and shrubs.

Hampshire

Bramdean House, Alresford	Of botanical interest, with specially fine herbaceous borders.
Chilworth Manor, Chilworth	Woodlands surrounding gardens and integral part of them. Trees, conifers, rhododendrons and azaleas.

Coles, Petersfield	Large garden of botanical interest. Water gardens with lily pool, ponds and bog plants. Woodland setting for rhododendrons. Many old trees and interesting shrubs.
Exbury Gardens, Southampton	Most famous of rhododendron gardens, 200 acres planted with them among trees and shrubs. Wonderful bulb effects in spring. Lakes.
Jermyns House*, Ampfield	Scree garden, peat and bog gardens. Fine collection of trees and shrubs including conifers.
June, Christchurch	Tiny garden, but featuring interesting planting.
Lepe House, Exbury, Southampton	Woodland garden on the mouth of the river Beaulieu. Spring interest for rhododendrons.
Longstock Park Water Gardens, Stockbridge	A water garden of considerable range. Bog and water plants in a natural wooded setting. Rhododendrons, azaleas and oak trees.
Pylewell Park, Lymington	Garden of botanical interest. Rhododendrons and other flowering shrubs, in a woodland setting which stretches towards the Solent from the house and its surrounding formal garden.
Vineyard, Hambledon	Unique vineyard—for England. Lectures given and wine to be purchased. Small pleasure garden.

Herefordshire

Barrington Hall, Leominster	Landscape by 'Capability' Brown. Good herbaceous borders and wide views. (N.T.)
Croft Castle, Leominster	A Welsh border castle. Garden recently replanted to some extent and all plants labelled. Outstanding trees, especially the avenue of Spanish chestnuts.
Eastnor Castle, Ledbury	An impressive pile among large trees, including the first cedars ever to be planted in England. The castle stands above a lake with the Malvern Hills as a backdrop.

Hergest Croft Garden and Park Wood, Kington	Trees, some conifers of great size are surrounded by rhododendrons and other flowering shrubs in this extensive garden.

Hertfordshire

Ashridge, Berkhamsted	Lawns, rhododendrons, small rock garden, monks' garden. (Amid N.T. park but not owned by the Trust).
Fanhams Hall*, Ware	Trees, old formal garden, remarkable Japanese garden constructed by Japanese designers. Botanically interesting.
Hatfield House, Hatfield	Great formal garden on large scale. Parterre, maze, statuary and balustrades, trees.
Julians, Rushden	Well planted garden of shrubs, herbaceous plants, climbers. Old walled garden. Lily pool with bronze seal fountain, trees, birds, herbs, thyme walk.
Knebworth House, Knebworth	Formal garden. Pleached limes of considerable interest. Roses, herbaceous borders.
St. Paul's Waldenbury, Hitchin	Informal flower and shrub garden. Temples and clipped beech hedges form an eighteenth century formal garden. Old orangery, water garden. Of botanical interest.

Kent

*Bedgebury National Pinetum, Goudhurst	An extension of the Royal Botanic Gardens, Kew, where the national collection of conifers is housed. Everything labelled. Well planned. Lake.
Chartwell, Westerham	Lake with black swans, water garden, good pergola, kitchen garden and rose garden. (N.T.)
Chilham Castle, Canterbury	Old walls, topiary, ancient mulberry tree. Terraces, statuary and fountain.
Crittenden House, Matfield	Contemporary garden around old house, has been planned along labour-saving lines. Water garden in old iron workings, old orchards linking the simple garden with the woodland beyond.
Godington Park, Ashford	Trees, formal gardens with topiary and yew edges. Italianate influence in design.

Hever Castle, Edenbridge	Castle was the home of Anne Boleyn. Enormous lake of 35 acres. Old moat garden. Rhododendron walk, rock garden, water garden with cascades. Superb Italian garden, one of the finest examples in the country. Topiary chessmen. Maze, avenues, views.
Hole Park, Rolvenden	Spring garden for naturalised bulbs, rhododendrons and azaleas. Water garden in woodland setting. Formal with roses and herbaceous borders and yew hedges.
Leeds Castle, Maidstone	Eighteenth century landscape gardens. Castle on an island. Good at daffodil time.
Lullingstone Castle, Eynsford	Lawns with decorative borders, herb garden, lake.
Knole, Sevenoaks	Landscaped garden and deer park. (N.T.)
Mereworth Castle, Maidstone	Lawns, herbaceous borders, yew walks.
Northbourne Court, Deal	Brick terraces and steps provide a soft background for choice shrubs and perennials. Grey leaved plants. Walled garden of some age. Mount.
Penshurst Place, Tunbridge Wells	Parts of the house date from the fourteenth century and the formal garden had its origin in the sixteenth century.
Scotney Castle, Lamberhurst	Specially recommended for autumn colour. A woodland garden surrounding a wide moated castle.
Sissinghurst Castle, Sissinghurst	A famous garden created by the late V. Sackville West, moat, several gardens, a profusion of roses, a silver-leaved garden, herb garden and pleached lime walk. (N.T.)
Sissinghurst Court, Cranbrook	Azaleas, rhododendrons, flowering cherries, herbaceous borders and yew hedges behind them. Water garden with fountain
Sissinghurst Place, Tenterden	Small garden made within the ruined four walls of a burnt-out house, provides a home for tender plants. Large Durmast oak.

Lancashire

Cranford, Aughton
: A tiny garden, exquisitely planned within the owners occupation of the house. Good shrubs and interesting planting schemes.

Holker Hall, Cartmel
: Shrubs and trees. Some unusual for the north.

Leicestershire

Baggrave Hall, Hungarton
: Sunken garden and water garden, trees and herbaceous border.

Brooksbury Agricultural College, Melton Mowbray
: Lake and water garden, demonstration plots; everything named.

Prestwold Hall, Loughborough
: Roses in number, trees, woodland garden, herbaceous plants, conservatory, and lawns. Extensive gardens.

Sedgemere, Market Bosworth
: Natural rock and water garden in a woodland setting. Best in spring and early summer.

Lincolnshire

Gunby Hall, Skegness
: Formal garden, lawns with magnificent cedars, moat, old walled garden. (N.T.)

Harrington Hall, Spilsby
: Roses, herbaceous borders, brooms. Not a very big garden.

Marston Hall, Grantham
: Old garden, mixed planting, some good trees.

Thorpe Hall, Louth
: Walled garden, dovecote, both dating from the sixteenth century, large rose garden. Parkland watered by attractive stream.

Well Vale, Alford
: Parkland, lake, flowering cherries and bulbs in spring.

Greater London

Danson Park, Bexley Heath
: Parkland with boating lake water and rock garden.

Derry & Toms Roof Garden, Kensington
: Period garden constructed a depth of 2½ft. of soil. Water, fountains, trees, container plants, wall plants.

Chiswick House, Chiswick
: Statuary, formality, Italian garden, conservatories, trees including cedars. Buildings of taste, river.

Fulham Palace, S.W.6
: 18 acres, trees, courtyard enclosed by Tudor buildings, central fountain.

Hall Place, Bexley	Parkland with conservatories roses, water garden.
Hampton Court	Immense formal garden, largely faithfully reconstructed, fountains, water, knot garden, clipped hedges, flower gardens and maze.
Kensington Palace, Kensington	Orangery, pleached limes, round pond, trees.
Lambeth Palace, S.E.1	10 acres. Ancient terrace and one or two old trees, paving, grass and flower beds.
Norwood Hall, Norwood Green	Now the Institute of Horticultural and Agricultural Education. Informal garden with comprehensive planting greenhouses, and demonstration plots.
Osterley Park, Osterley	Parkland, lake, trees, herbaceous plants (N.T.)
Syon Park, (The Gardening Centre) Brentford	Trees, river, old site rejuvenated to form a gardeners' showplace for horticulture in Britain. **Permanent exhibitions.**

Norfolk

Blickling Hall, Aylsham	Large formal garden with topiary avenue through rhododendrons to a classical temple. Lake, trees. Good garden ornaments. (N.T.)
Bressingham Hall, Diss	An informal layout with lawns, water and dell garden. The finest collection in the country of herbaceous perennials (many of them raised here).
Holkham Hall*, Wells	Formal garden of considerable importance laid out by Barry. Terraces, topiary, box edges, fountains, trees, many of them unusual.
Lammas Hall*, Norwich	Medium sized garden, with an abundance of spring flowers and bulbs and a young arboretum.
Oxburgh Hall, Swaffham	Fascinating moated house with 80ft. high gatehouse. Remarkable French parterre. (N.T.)
Raveningham Hall, Norwich	Extensive lawns and herbaceous borders, good perennials, yew hedges and trees.

Sandringham	An informal garden although set along geometric lines. Brick walls, terraces, roses, water and rock garden, glasshouses.
Shadwell Park, Thetford	Walled garden, good trees, lawns.
South Pickenham Hall, Swaffham	River and lake, lawns, herbaceous borders, greenhouses, walled garden, wild fowl.
Swanington Manor, Norwich	Topiary and 400 year-old yews, roses and herbaceous beds.
Talbot Manor, Fincham	The largest collection of plants, many of them tender, in private ownership in this country.

Northamptonshire

Barnwell Manor, Oundle	Formal garden around ruined castle, trees and shrubs and lily pool.
Cotterstock Hall, Oundle	Water gardens and herbaceous borders, trees and shrubs.
Cottesbrooke Hall, Northampton	Unusual formal garden, with small courtyards, trees and wild garden beyond.
Easton Neston* Towcester	Large formal garden, walled garden, water, arboretum.
Flore House, Northampton	Good trees, in parkland setting, mixed borders, greenhouses.
Grey Court, King's Sutton	Roses, water with stream, yew hedges. Unusual plants.
Moulton Grange, Pitsford	Landscape with lawns, lilies, water garden, interesting trees.
Rockingham Castle, Market Harborough	Old trees and yew hedges, commanding position above the Welland valley. Roses, herbaceous plants.
The Glebe House, Collingtree	Water garden, yew hedges, topiary, water, attractive in spring with bulbs and early flowers. Birds.

Northumberland

Eglingham Hall, Alnwick	Rhododendron collection, well labelled, heathers, lawns and bulbs.
Howick, Alnwick	Large garden of rhododendrons and other flowering shrubs.
Seaton Delaval Hall, Whitley Bay	Parkland with trees and shrubs.

Nottinghamshire

Babworth Hall, Retford	Landscape garden, laid out by Repton. Daffodils.
Morton Hall*, Retford	Trees, especially conifers, spring flowers, rhododendrons and azaleas.
Newstead Abbey, Nottingham	Large formal garden, extensive planting of rare trees and shrubs.
Thoresby Hall, Ollerton	Great Victorian setting for trees and shrubs.
Thrumpton Hall, Nottingham	Trees of special interest, planted to commemorate historical events since the time of George III. Formal garden and lake, walled garden and clipped yew hedges.

Oxfordshire

Blenheim Palace, Woodstock	Grandeur on a scale not to be seen elsewhere in England. Intricate parterre and water garden. Lake created by 'Capability' Brown. Spacious parkland.
Chastleton, Moreton-in-the-Marsh	Remains of seventeenth century topiary in box. Dovecote.
Haseley Court, Haseley	Informal planting in a formal setting. Courtyard, moat and remarkable topiary garden open to the surrounding views.
Oxford Botanic Gardens, Oxford	Old walls, glasshouses, rock and scree garden, water and river, trees. Botanical interest.
Oxford gardens	College gardens open to the public daily. Noteworthy walls, iron work, lawns, trees and shrubs and bedding plants. Occasionally the private gardens of some colleges are open, quietly enclosed in ancient buildings.
Rousham, Steeple Aston	Landscaped by William Kent and essentially as he planned it. Statuary, river and glades, temples and arcade, bowling green, dovecote, trees.
Tew Park, Great Tew	Lawns and small rock outcrop, walled gardens, gatehouse. Splendid trees hereabouts planted by Loudon.
Waterperry Horticultural College, Wheatley	Herbaceous borders, old walls, alpines, raised beds, fruit on model plots, greenhouses and kitchen garden.

Rutland

Exton Park, Oakham	Extensive parkland with good trees, lake, spring bulbs.
Holywell Hall, Stamford	Parkland sloping to lake, with fine trees, dovecote.
Kirby Hall, Uppingham	Seventeenth century garden, unearthed during contemporary reconstruction and restored.
The Old Hall, Langham	Courtyard with well head. Herbaceous plants and lilies, some unusual plants.

Shropshire

Attingham Park, Shrewsbury	Landscaped parkland with river. Work of Repton. (N.T.)
Burford House Gardens, Tenbury Wells	Well planted recently redesigned garden of medium size.
Hatton Grange, Shifnal	Water garden, rhododendrons, trees.
Hodnet Hall, Hodnet	Woodland garden with two lakes set among trees and rhododendrons and other flowering shrubs. Well designed for colour effect.
Ludstone Hall, Claverley	Moats and fishponds, both old. Interesting knot garden in clipped box represents playing cards.
Wenlock Abbey, Much Wenlock	Medium sized garden with walled rose garden on ancient abbey site.

Somerset and Bristol

Ammerdown Park, Radstock	Much of interest in this garden designed by Sir Edwin Lutyens. Yews, water, terraces, statuary, fountains, pergola and lime avenue.
Barrington Court, Ilminster	Charming old-world rose and iris gardens, spring bulbs, lilies, wall shrubs and lawns. (N.T.)
Bristol Zoological Gardens, Clifton	Trees and shrubs of interest. Rock garden, greenhouses including a tropical house.
Claverton Manor, Bath	American museum. Part of the garden is a reconstruction of George Washington's garden at Mount Vernon U.S.A. Terrace, well-designed herb garden.

Clevedon Court, Clevedon	Eighteenth century terraced gardens around an older house. Old octagonal summer house, trees, and herbaceous plants. (N.T.)
East Lambrook Manor, South Petherton	Informal garden of immense botanical interest among stone walls. Particular attention has been given to variety of leaf and texture in the planting. Read *We made a Garden* by Margery Fish —the story of the making of this garden.
Ellicombe, Minehead	Semi-formal garden with pools, Some interesting ironwork.
Montacute House, Langport	Formal walls with gazebos, trees, good views of surrounding countryside. (N.T.)
Orchardleigh Park, Frome	Large garden, terraces, lake, walled kitchen garden.
Prior Park, Bath	Landscape garden with water and noteworthy Palladian bridge.
Tintinhull House, Yeovil	Semi-formal garden, of mixed planting for good colour effect. Water garden with summer house, courtyard. (N.T.)
Underway, Porlock	Botanically interesting collection of trees and shrubs and bulbs.

Staffordshire

Alton Towers, Uttoxeter	Some good trees bring together a wide variety of style and features. Water, garden houses, fountains.
Blithfield, Rugely	Woodland and park with large oaks, roses, orangery.
Elds Wood, Willoughbridge	Wild garden created in old gravel quarry, interesting plants, rhododendrons and spring effect.
Sandon Hall, Great Haywood	Large garden with some good trees, roses, kitchen garden, amphitheatre.
Wightwick Manor, Wolverhampton	Formal terraced garden with topiary and yew hedges. (N.T.)

Suffolk

Heveningham Hall, Halesworth	Landscaped garden with good trees. Design attributed to 'Capability' Brown. Roses and herbaceous borders. Orangery by Wyatt.

Ickworth, Bury St. Edmunds	Formal garden with long terrace and yew hedges. Trees of considerable interest, unusual plants. (N.T.)
Little Thurlow Park, Haverhill	Four acre walled garden, water garden with two moats, roses and trees.
Melford Hall, Long Melford	Enormous walled garden and octagonal garden house. (N.T.)
Somerleyton Hall, Lowestoft	Trees and an avenue, maze well-planted with connoisseur's plants.

Surrey

Ashburton House, Send	Lawns running down to river and streams. Bulbs naturalised, rhododendrons and azaleas, greenhouse.
Chilworth Manor, Guildford	Informal garden planned around an old seventeenth century garden. Old walls and terrace.
Dunsborough Park, Ripley	Formal rose garden, herbaceous borders, rock and water garden, topiary, fruit under glass.
Grayswood Hill, Haslemere	Fine trees and shrubs, rhododendrons and azaleas; irises in midsummer and hydrangeas in late-summer. Delightful garden.
Hascombe Court, Godalming	Collection of trees and flowering shrubs including rhododendrons. Spring bulbs in profusion, rock garden, formal water garden.
Ockham Mill, Ripley	Formal garden by old mill stream, herbaceous plants.
Polesden Lacey, Dorking	Trees, especially beech, walls, roses, herbaceous plants. Terraced to give good views of surrounding hills. (N.T.)
Pyrford Court, Pyrford	Herbaceous borders, shrubs.
Royal Botanic Gardens, Kew	Almost every style of gardening, glasshouses. Immense botanical interest combined with beauty. Garden buildings.
Sutton Place, Guildford	Extensive lawns, Dutch garden.
Winkworth Arboretum*, Godalming	A collection of trees planted on a hillside. Of great interest at all times of the year. (N.T.)

Wisley*, Ripley	The garden of the Royal Horticultural Society. Wild and woodland garden well planted with bulbs and woodland plants. Lake, heather garden, pinetum, shrub collections. Rhododendrons and azaleas on Battleston Hill. Collection of flowering cherries. Newly renovated rock and water garden.

Sussex

Batemans, Burwash	A formal garden on different levels, planned by Rudyard Kipling. Roses, pool, pleached alley, yews. (N.T.)
Borde Hill, Haywards Heath	Modern informal garden of botanical interest. Good trees and shrubs especially plants from western China. Greenhouse.
Field Place, Horsham	Shelley's birthplace. Woodland setting for water plants, informal garden with lawns and herbaceous plants around house.
Great Dixter, Northiam	Formal gardens, with much stone work, walls, topiary, herbaceous perennials *par excellence*.
Heaselands, Haywards Heath	Water garden, trees and shrubs and woodland garden, roses, aviary and some wild fowl.
Highdown, Goring-by-Sea	A remarkable garden made in a chalk pit. Exquisite mixed planting of flowering plants.
Leonardslea, Horsham	Trees and shrubs in an extensive woodland garden lush with rhododendrons, azaleas, magnolias and other flowering trees and shrubs, Water, small lakes.
Nymans*, Crawley	Walls, especially walls of ruined house and courtyard planted with good shrubs. Topiary, heather garden and rock garden. Pinetum. (N.T.)
Sedgwick Park, Horsham	Yew hedges surround formal garden of considerable proportion, water garden and roses.
Sheffield Park, Uckfield	Trees in a parkland setting with five lakes descending the hillside. Magnificent autumn colour. (N.T.)
Sunte House, Haywards Heath	Water garden and woodland setting for rhododendrons, magnolias and flowering shrubs generally.

Sutton End, Petworth	Informal garden with stone work, low growing plants, alpines, conifers.
Wakehurst Place, Ardingly	A woodland garden with lakes, set on a hillside.

Warwickshire

Arbury Hall, Nuneaton	Parkland and landscaped gardens with many trees, some of them in avenues along carriage ways
Birmingham Botanic Gardens	Large rock garden, several greenhouses including cacti house. Trees and shrubs.
Charlecote Park, Stratford-upon-Avon	Tudor gatehouse, and avenue parkland. Deer (N.T.)
Compton Wynyates, Banbury	Set in the hollow of surrounding hills. An interesting topiary garden, with bedding plants. Tudor house noteworthy.
Farnborough Hall, Banbury	Good views from a long terraced walk and two temples, obelisk. (N.T.)
Packwood House, Hockley Heath	Famous topiary garden said to represent the Sermon on the Mount. Walls of interest, with gateway and bee boles; old heating flues in walls for fruit growing in former days. (N.T.)
Stratford-upon-Avon gardens	Attractive gardens at Shakespeare's birthplace, includes the plants mentioned in his work; Elizabethan style knot garden at New Place; cottage style garden at Ann Hathaway's cottage.
Upton House, Edgehill, Banbury	A lawn surrounds the house, and beyond is a formal garden, terraced to a long pool at the bottom. (N.T.)
Warwick Castle, Warwick	Formal garden surrounded by parkland first laid out by 'Capability' Brown. Good trees.

Westmorland

Dallam Tower, Milnthorpe	Natural rock garden with waterfalls, woodland and shrubs, fine climbing roses and rose garden.
Levens Hall, Kendal	Unique in England for its age and topiary and adherence to the original plan. Avenue of oaks in danger from road development.

Sizergh Castle, Kendal	Rock and water garden with outstanding collection of ferns. (N.T.)

Wiltshire

Corsham Court, Chippenham	Good trees in landscape planned by 'Capability' Brown.
Fonthill House, Tisbury	Extensive garden with fine trees, herbaceous borders, sunken garden and formal bedding, rhododendrons in spring.
Fyfield Manor, Pewsey	Garden of medium size with much colour, roses and herbaceous plants, herb garden.
Hungerdown House, Chippenham	Lime tolerant plants in number. Roses, shrubs. Contemporary formal garden with fountain, shrub roses.
Iford Manor, Bradford-on-Avon	Terraced garden with much stonework and statuary and items of interest to students of Peto. Cloisters, marbles and bronzes.
Lackham School of Agriculture (Lacock Abbey), Chippenham	Large gardens, walled garden, greenhouses, demonstration plots, mixed borders of shrubs and perennials, museum of old farm and garden implements.
Lake House, Salisbury	Informal garden and woodland setting. Shrubs, roses, water, pleached limes.
Stourhead, Mere	Probably the most outstanding landscape garden in England. Lake, trees, temples, rhododendrons. (N.T.)
West Kington House, Chippenham	Essentially a water garden planned on a hillside in a trout stream valley; roses.
Wilbury Park, Newton Tony	Medium sized garden among pinewoods. Grotto, eighteenth century temple.
Wilton House, Salisbury	Lawns down to the river on a level site, cedar trees. Palladian bridge, statuary.

Worcestershire

Davenham, Malvern	Garden of botanical interest, trees, shrubs and alpines.
Orchard House, Broadway	Formal manor house garden. Bulbs, water garden and topiary.

Rous Lench Court, Evesham	Famous topiary of cumbersome proportions, stone stairway lined by thick yew hedges.
Spetchley Park, Worcester	Parkland setting for trees, with naturalised daffodils. Deer.

Yorkshire

Bramham Park, Boston Spa	A water garden with canals, fountains and cascades. Beech trees of some age.
Burnby Gardens, Pocklington	Lily ponds of immense size in a country setting.
Burton Agnes, Bridlington	Elizabethan courtyard planted with topiary. Otherwise modern semi-formal garden.
Castle Howard, Malton	A water garden of the eighteenth century with bridge, mausoleum, temple, statuary of exquisite proportions.
Duncombe Park, Helmsley	Formal garden with important curved terrace above the river Rye, with a temple at each end. Above and integral with Rievaulx Abbey.
Fountains Abbey and Studley Royal, Ripon	Picturesque setting for a water garden on a large scale. Lakes, temples. Monastic ruins.
Harewood House, Harrogate	A terraced formal garden surrounded by parkland. Aviary being built.
Harlow Car, Harrogate	The garden of the Northern Horticultural Society. Woodland and informal garden with much colour and well considered planting.
Newby Hall, Skelton	Garden of botanical interest. Herbaceous borders, hedges, water and rock gardens.
Nostell Priory, Wakefield	Parkland and informal planting, boating on the lake. House has some important pieces of furniture. (N.T.)
St. Nicholas, Richmond	A garden of outstanding merit, containing many plants not normally grown in Yorkshire. Many wall plants, hedges and herbaceous borders.
Sledmere House, Driffield	Italianate design with extensive lawns. Parkland originally by 'Capability' Brown. Walled rose garden.
Thorpe Perrow*, Bedale	Large garden, wild garden and lake with swans, trees.

Two other books for garden lovers

Discovering Topiary by Margaret Baker (4/6d.) is a history of the art of topiary with chapters on the choice of suitable trees and shrubs, their cultivation and clipping, and a county list of gardens in which topiary may be seen.

Zoos, Bird Gardens & Animal Collections in Great Britain and Eire (5/-) lists over 120 places with full details of opening times, admission fees, exhibits and special attractions. Many are set out in established parks and gardens; others show skilful use of planting to achieve natural effects for the creatures that are kept there.

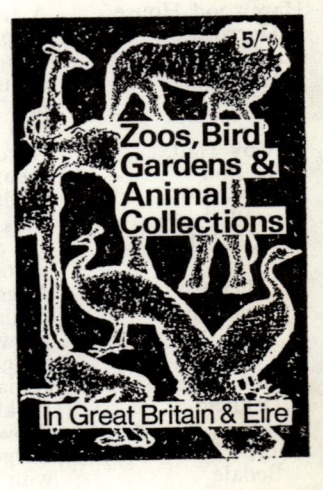